Reading Skills
3-4

Written by
Trisha Callella

Editor: Carla Hamaguchi
Illustrator: Jenny Campbell
Designer/Production: Moonhee Pak/Mary Gagné
Cover Designer: Barbara Peterson
Art Director: Tom Cochrane
Project Director: Carolea Williams

Table of Contents

Introduction

Each book in the *Power Practice*™ series contains over 100 ready-to-use activity pages to provide students with skill practice. The fun activities can be used to supplement and enhance what you are teaching in your classroom. Give an activity page to students as independent class work, or send the pages home as homework to reinforce skills taught in class. An answer key is provided for quick reference.

The practical and creative activities in *Reading Skills 3–4* give students the perfect way to practice and reinforce over 20 reading skills including

- inferences
- drawing conclusions
- context clues
- sequencing
- predicting
- making connections
- following and comprehending directions
- main idea
- summarizing
- cause and effect
- point of view

Use these ready-to-go activities to "recharge" skill review and give students the power to succeed!

Reading Skills 3–4 • © 2004 Creative Teaching Press

Add 'Em Up!

COMPOUND WORDS

A **compound word** is a word formed with two or more words.
  Example: chalk + board = chalkboard

Fill in the missing word in each "compound word equation".

1 barn + _____ = a place where farm animals live

2 _____ + bone = your spinal cord which helps you stand up straight

3 court + _____ = the location of a trial

4 _____ + ball = a popular sport played on a field where players score touchdowns

5 _____ + work = what you do to practice what you've learned

6 pine + _____ = something that grows on a tree and provides food for forest animals

7 _____ + wear = something that is worn beneath the clothing

8 scare + _____ = something you might find guarding crops at a farm

9 _____ + proof = what an item is described as being if it can get wet without being damaged

10 suit + _____ = a carrier for clothing on trips

11 _____ + stroke = a form of swimming

12 _____ + house = a transparent building where plants are grown

Compound Crossword

COMPOUND WORDS

Use compound words to complete the crossword puzzle.

Across
1. something worn on a person's back to carry books and materials
2. a type of boat that requires wind
4. a person on duty at a pool
5. a very tall building named because it seems to brush up against the sky
7. the opposite of outdoor
9. a hard layer on the end of a finger
11. a container for tea

Down
3. a natural disaster; a shaking or trembling of the ground
6. what is turned on a door to open it
8. printed sheets of paper that contain news and interesting stories
12. recess location

Reading Skills 3–4 • © 2004 Creative Teaching Press

Name _____ Date _____

Compound Word Search

COMPOUND WORDS

Find and circle compound words from the word box in the word search. Then look for 8 more compound words in the puzzle. List the words you find and circle them in the puzzle.

birdhouse	blueberry	watercolor	wastebasket
smokestack	cupcake	fisherman	bathtub

u	n	d	e	r	w	e	a	r	b	i	r	d	h	o	u	s	e	l	b
x	e	a	u	n	a	m	r	e	h	s	i	f	c	b	z	t	w	e	d
v	i	i	m	k	u	l	m	v	o	t	a	c	x	m	e	o	d	k	x
b	k	v	j	w	v	m	g	i	i	b	j	u	f	o	e	r	j	c	u
l	o	h	l	l	n	o	h	n	p	l	k	p	b	k	o	y	t	i	j
u	f	o	c	s	m	o	k	e	s	t	a	c	k	o	p	b	m	m	k
e	g	n	k	b	k	n	y	y	n	r	y	a	m	n	w	o	f	a	r
b	y	y	s	m	o	s	c	a	o	f	q	k	a	c	a	o	n	e	o
e	a	c	a	p	a	r	s	r	w	m	l	e	d	b	q	k	n	r	l
r	w	z	j	q	b	r	t	d	s	h	o	a	z	z	x	a	y	d	o
r	l	w	r	f	a	u	k	l	t	w	a	w	g	g	l	d	e	y	c
y	l	a	h	p	t	r	r	q	o	b	p	i	i	p	h	h	e	a	r
q	a	e	s	t	h	s	y	x	r	d	f	o	r	i	o	w	d	d	e
t	h	a	l	f	t	i	m	e	m	n	j	i	g	c	b	l	y	e	t
g	z	v	u	b	u	s	r	x	f	g	a	u	p	h	u	c	e	z	a
w	a	s	t	e	b	a	s	k	e	t	e	q	f	x	b	t	a	k	w

Words I found:

Compound Collections

COMPOUND WORDS

The word box contains words that can be combined in many different ways to make compound words. Use these words to write as many compound words as you can.

less	over	stood	time	under	many
light	any	some	place	ground	use
end	head	go	more	hear	ever

_____   _____   _____

_____   _____   _____

_____   _____   _____

_____   _____   _____

_____   _____   _____

_____   _____   _____

Reading Skills 3–4 • © 2004 Creative Teaching Press

Name _____ Date _____

Simple Similes

FIGURATIVE LANGUAGE

> A **simile** is a comparison of two unlike things, using the connecting words *like* or *as*.
> Example: She was as sly as a fox.
> She was clever and sneaky, so she was compared to a fox.

Underline the similes in the following sentences.

1. He was as funny as a comedian.

2. She was as hungry as a horse.

3. They were as wild as a pair of monkeys.

4. He acted like a frightened rabbit.

5. Isn't that painting as colorful as a rainbow?

6. The players were as fast as an airplane.

7. His letter was as priceless as a treasure.

8. She was as smart as a teacher.

9. The experiment was as explosive as a volcano.

10. She was like an elephant the way she ate so many peanuts.

11. The baby was as cute as a button.

12. Joey thought the job was as easy as pie.

13. Kim felt as sick as a dog after she ate ten hot dogs.

14. Playing chess with my dad is like trying to outsmart a computer.

15. Billy was as stubborn as a mule.

Simile Match-Up

FIGURATIVE LANGUAGE

Write the letter of the word that best completes each simile.

1. _____ as fast as
2. _____ as big as
3. _____ as smooth as
4. _____ as cold as
5. _____ as quiet as
6. _____ as loud as
7. _____ as tiny as
8. _____ as light as
9. _____ as hard as
10. _____ as sly as
11. _____ as funny as
12. _____ as brave as
13. _____ as colorful as
14. _____ as gloomy as
15. _____ as bright as

a. a fox

b. silk

c. a stereo

d. a warrior

e. an ant

f. a rock

g. a cheetah

h. a comic book

i. ice

j. a feather

k. a sunny day

l. an elephant

m. a rainbow

n. a cloudy day

o. a mouse

Reading Skills 3–4 • © 2004 Creative Teaching Press

Metaphors

FIGURATIVE LANGUAGE

A **metaphor** is a comparison that does not use connecting words.
  Example: A smile is the doorway to happiness.
  A smile is not really a doorway, but when you smile it makes you feel happier.

Underline the two items being compared in each sentence. Write what the sentence really means.

1 Your education is the gateway to success.

_____

2 Her life is a roller coaster of events.

_____

3 Dad's beard was a prickly porcupine.

_____

4 His mother thought he was being a pain in the neck.

_____

5 She said, "My brother is such a clown."

_____

6 Chris was a walking encyclopedia.

_____

7 The shy girl became a graceful swan when she danced.

_____

8 We would have had more to eat if Tyler hadn't been such a hog.

_____

Simile or Metaphor

FIGURATIVE LANGUAGE

Read each sentence. Circle **S** if the sentence is a simile or **M** if it contains a metaphor.

1 The sunburned girl was as red as a beet.   S   M

2 It's an oven in this room!   S   M

3 She would not give in because, she was as stubborn as a mule.   S   M

4 His brain is a factory that always comes up with ideas.   S   M

5 Life is like a bowl of cherries.   S   M

6 His room was a pigsty.   S   M

7 The weightlifter was as strong as an ox.   S   M

8 It's a jungle on the playground right now.   S   M

9 The sand is the carpet of the ocean.   S   M

10 Her skin was as smooth as silk.   S   M

11 The directions you gave us were crystal clear.   S   M

12 When it came to getting shots, he was such a chicken.   S   M

13 The criminal was as sly as a fox.   S   M

14 I spent two hours cleaning the house so it was
as clean as a whistle.   S   M

15 The leftover pizza was as hard as a stone.   S   M

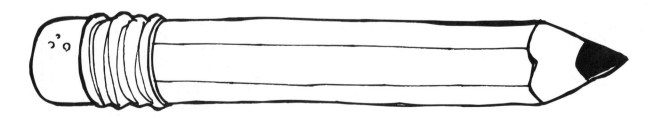

Reading Skills 3–4 • © 2004 Creative Teaching Press

Hooray for Homophones

HOMOPHONES

> **Homophones** are words that have the same sound but are spelled differently and have different meanings.
> Example: threw/through
> Keith <u>threw</u> the ball to Shiloh.
> Keith walked <u>through</u> the museum in Paris.

Write the homophone for each word.

1 hole _____

2 there _____

3 witch _____

4 hear _____

5 knight _____

6 not _____

7 clothes _____

8 daze _____

9 deer _____

10 sighed _____

Circle the correct homophone in each sentence.

11 The game was (tied/tide) at the end of the first quarter.

12 By the end of the (weak/week), she had cleaned her (whole/hole) house.

13 What (would/wood) you like for dessert?

14 He (red/read) the book in two (days/daze).

15 Would you like me to help you (pour/poor) that water?

16 Let's (paws/pause) for a moment of silence.

17 Her favorite team (one/won) the game!

18 Do you have any (led/lead) for my pencil?

Name _____ Date _____

Homophone Crossword Fun

Homophones

Read the sentences. Use the correct homophones to complete the crossword puzzle.

Across

1. The _____ of her perfume made me sneeze.
2. A penny is worth one _____.
3. We rode a _____ to get to the Statue of Liberty.
4. The tooth _____ left money under my pillow.
5. Whom did you _____ for the job?
6. The rate increase made my monthly bill _____ than it was before.
7. The morning _____ on the plants and flowers sparkled in the sunlight.
8. Your library book is _____ in three days.

Down

3. The airplane _____ from Los Angeles to New York.
4. I had all the symptoms of the ____: fever, headache, and fatigue.
6. I covered the _____ in my pants with a patch.
9. They ate the _____ pizza and did not save me a piece.
10. They hitched the boat to the back of the truck and _____ it to the river.
11. A ____ is an animal that is like a frog.

Reading Skills 3–4 • © 2004 Creative Teaching Press

What Does It Mean?

HOMOPHONES

Write the letter of the definition that matches each homophone.

1 _____ allowed

2 _____ aloud

3 _____ flea

4 _____ flee

5 _____ flour

6 _____ flower

7 _____ hair

8 _____ hare

9 _____ plane

10 _____ plain

11 _____ doe

12 _____ dough

13 _____ heard

14 _____ herd

15 _____ ant

16 _____ aunt

a. a small insect that lives in colonies

b. a very thin, threadlike growth on the skin of people and animals

c. a group of animals

d. a female deer

e. common or ordinary

f. an insect that feeds on the blood of humans and animals

g. a fine meal that is made by grinding grains

h. a thick mixture of ingredients used to make bread

i. the sister of one's mother or father

j. to have permission to do or have something

k. to have received sound through the ears

l. an animal that is like a rabbit

m. to run away

n. an aircraft

o. the part of a plant that has colored petals

p. out loud

Name _____ Date _____

Unscramble It

HOMOPHONES

> **Homophones** are words that have the same sound but are spelled differently and have different meanings.
> Example: read/red
> She <u>read</u> her favorite book again.
> The <u>red</u> shirt was her favorite.

Complete each sentence with a homophone. Unscramble the letters at the end of the sentence if you need help.

1. She needed to _____ up her antique clock in order for it to work. (niwd)

2. He _____ when he didn't get his way, but it never worked. (nhdiwe)

3. Can you see that huge _____ in the garden? If you touch it, you'll get warts! (daot)

4. The truck _____ the car to the nearest service station to be repaired. (wotde)

5. Do you enjoy listening to fairy _____. (altse)

6. Animal lovers enjoy seeing the _____ wag on their pets. (tslia)

7. Did you enjoy the last _____ of the movie? (seenc)

8. Have you _____ my wallet? I can't seem to find it. (eens)

9. The sun's _____ were shining brightly. (ysar)

10. Her mom was so excited when she got her _____. It meant a bigger paycheck. (rseia)

Reading Skills 3–4 • © 2004 Creative Teaching Press

Paired Up

SYNONYMS AND ANTONYMS

Synonyms are words that have the same meaning.
> Example: big and large
> They both describe a similar size.

Write a synonym in the blank shoe to make each pair of shoes a pair of synonyms.

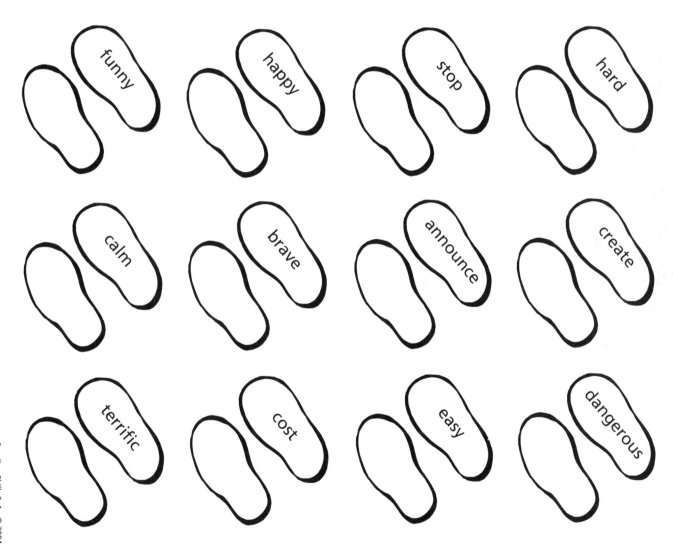

Super Sentences

Synonyms and Antonyms

Changing simple words to different synonyms often improves writing. In each of the following sentences, write a synonym for the underlined word.

1 _____ He thought the cupcakes tasted <u>good</u>.

2 _____ Her sister needed <u>help</u> getting up the stairs.

3 _____ The test questions seemed <u>hard</u> to him.

4 _____ She felt <u>happy</u> on her first day of school.

5 _____ It was <u>cold</u> at the beach.

6 _____ Jacob was <u>nice</u> to Trenton at recess.

7 _____ Danielle told her mother that she looked <u>pretty</u> in her new dress.

8 _____ Many people <u>like</u> going to the movies on weekends.

9 _____ He was very <u>fast</u> in the race.

10 _____ The large bag was too <u>big</u> to fit under the seat on the plane.

11 _____ She did a <u>super</u> job organizing her desk.

12 _____ The friends had a <u>fun</u> time at the circus.

13 _____ He laughed when he realized his <u>silly</u> mistake.

14 _____ The <u>gift</u> was wrapped with a huge red bow.

15 _____ He still needed to <u>finish</u> his homework.

Reading Skills 3–4 • © 2004 Creative Teaching Press

Antonym Crossword

SYNONYMS AND ANTONYMS

Read the clues. Use antonyms to complete the crossword puzzle.

Across
1. question
2. crooked
3. below
4. go
6. short
8. win
10. cry
11. far

day

night

Down
1. child
3. before
4. brother
5. quiet
7. north
8. right (direction)
9. false
10. first

Antonym Match-Up

SYNONYMS AND ANTONYMS

Antonyms are words that have opposite meanings.
    Example: empty and full

Match each word in the left column to the correct antonym from the right column.
Write the letter on the line.

1 _____ give   **a.** present

2 _____ plain   **b.** dirty

3 _____ different   **c.** fancy

4 _____ hard   **d.** forget

5 _____ rough   **e.** soft

6 _____ past   **f.** lose

7 _____ find   **g.** messy

8 _____ over   **h.** take

9 _____ light   **i.** under

10 _____ generous   **j.** save

11 _____ arrive   **k.** selfish

12 _____ clean   **l.** same

13 _____ organized   **m.** depart

14 _____ remember   **n.** smooth

15 _____ spend   **o.** dark

Reading Skills 3–4 • © 2004 Creative Teaching Press

Name _____ Date _____

Find the Synonyms and Antonyms

SYNONYMS AND ANTONYMS

Look at each word. Bubble in the correct **synonym**.

1 false	○ true	○ untrue	○ correct
2 healthy	○ well	○ sick	○ ill
3 aid	○ hinder	○ assist	○ cool
4 easy	○ simple	○ smooth	○ difficult
5 cheap	○ inexpensive	○ free	○ costly
6 filthy	○ dirty	○ clean	○ immaculate
7 wrong	○ incorrect	○ correct	○ right
8 caution	○ fragile	○ strong	○ warn
9 desire	○ help	○ want	○ hurt

Look at each word. Bubble in the correct **antonym**.

10 expire	○ subscribe	○ fire	○ renew
11 deny	○ lie	○ admit	○ help
12 fix	○ mend	○ sew	○ break
13 permanent	○ temporary	○ forever	○ ink
14 few	○ some	○ little	○ many
15 run	○ sprint	○ jog	○ walk
16 finish	○ start	○ complete	○ end
17 sum	○ add	○ multiply	○ difference
18 kind	○ mean	○ friendly	○ type

Name _____ Date _____

Solve the Riddle

FOLLOWING DIRECTIONS

Follow the directions to find the answer to the riddle.

How do you keep a skunk from smelling?

- Write the letter **a** on line 6.
- Write the word **plug** on line 2.
- Write the word **with** on line 5.
- Write the word **You** on line 1.
- Write the word **its** on line 3.
- Write the word **clothespin** on line 7.
- Write the word **nose** on line 4.

1 _____

2 _____

3 _____

4 _____

5 _____

6 _____

7 _____

Reading Skills 3–4 • © 2004 Creative Teaching Press

Hidden Truck

FOLLOWING DIRECTIONS

A truck is hidden in the squares. Follow the directions to find the truck.

Color all the squares with a consonant blue.
Color all the squares with a consonant blend green.
Color all the squares with a number black.
Color all the squares with a ◆ yellow.

e	i	o	dd	u	i	ef	a	fp	u
a	u	e	i	b	d	f	h	p	r
lh	zs	tw	tr	m	k	j	s	g	l
e	o	gr	cr	n	g	d	p	h	r
mn	a	cl	br	v	t	q	k	n	s
◆	ch	sw	dr	d	j	f	s	g	c
u	st	19	bl	m	w	z	b	4	f
kk	6	42	2	vw	zx	bg	8	5	9
rr	ih	3	i	wq	a	op	u	11	hj
kd	e	ns	ou	o	fd	u	tz	i	pp

Name _____ Date _____

Sports

FOLLOWING DIRECTIONS

basketball	tennis	hockey	soccer	volleyball
football	gymnastics	baseball	golf	surfing

Write the sports words in alphabetical order in Column A. Write the name of something associated with each sport in Column B. For example, for baseball you could write "mitt."

<table>
<tr><td align="center">Column A</td><td align="center">Column B</td></tr>
<tr><td>_____</td><td>_____</td></tr>
<tr><td>_____</td><td>_____</td></tr>
<tr><td>_____</td><td>_____</td></tr>
<tr><td>_____</td><td>_____</td></tr>
<tr><td>_____</td><td>_____</td></tr>
<tr><td>_____</td><td>_____</td></tr>
<tr><td>_____</td><td>_____</td></tr>
<tr><td>_____</td><td>_____</td></tr>
<tr><td>_____</td><td>_____</td></tr>
</table>

What's My Name?

Following Directions

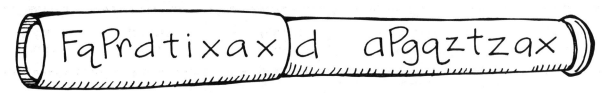

FqPrdtixax d aPgaztzax

Follow each step in order to find the name of a famous explorer. Write your final answer on the lines at the bottom of the page.

1 Change all the **x's** to **n's.**

2 Cross out all the **P's.**

3 Add an **M** to the beginning of the second word.

4 Change all the **q's** to **e's.**

5 Change all the **z's** to **l's.**

6 Cross out all the **t's.**

The explorer is

___ ___ ___ ___ ___ ___ ___ ___ ___

___ ___ ___ ___ ___ ___ ___ ___

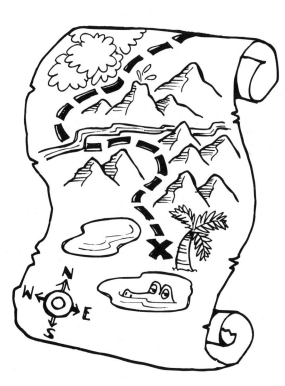

What Tools Do We Need?

ANALOGIES

An **analogy** is a relationship between two pairs of words. One type of analogy relates tools to the people who use them.
Example: farmer : hoe : : carpenter : hammer

Fill in the missing tool or worker to complete each analogy.

1 construction worker : _____ : : custodian : vacuum

2 _____ : gavel : : navigator : compass

3 potter : wheel : : _____ : loom

4 electrician : wires : : librarian : _____

5 firefighter : ladder : : _____ : test tube

6 referee : _____ : : sculptor : chisel

7 chef : _____ : : waitress : tray

8 welder : torch : : gardener : _____

9 dentist : drill : : _____ : stethoscope

10 _____ : clippers : : scientist : microscope

11 _____ : pen : : artist : paint

12 _____ : anchor : : massage therapist : table

13 _____ : mop : : mathematician : calculator

14 typist : keyboard : : _____ : microphone

Write three of your own worker—tool analogies.

1 _____ : _____ : : _____ : _____

2 _____ : _____ : : _____ : _____

3 _____ : _____ : : _____ : _____

Reading Skills 3–4 • © 2004 Creative Teaching Press

Name _____ Date _____

Synonym and Antonym Analogies

Aɴᴀʟᴏɢɪᴇs

A **synonym analogy** compares two sets of words. Each set is a synonym pair.
   Example: infant : baby : : seat : chair
   An infant is a baby just like a seat is a chair.
An **antonym analogy** compares two sets of words. Each set is an antonym pair.
   Example: big : small : : funny : sad. Big is the opposite of small just like funny is the
   opposite of sad.

Write the word that best completes each analogy.

1 puzzled : confused : : _____ : joyful

2 lift : _____ : : stop : finish

3 answer : respond : : _____ : irritate

4 true : false : : empty : _____

5 before : after : : _____ : late

6 write : _____ : : listen : hear

7 problem : _____ : : comedy : tragedy

8 _____ : locate : : sell : peddle

9 fancy : plain : : expensive : _____

10 automobile : _____ : : taxi : cab

11 succeed : fail : : _____ : quit

12 selfish : generous : : _____ : quiet

13 happy : glad : : _____ : mad

14 dry : _____ : : neat : messy

Name _____ Date _____

Grammar Analogies

ANALOGIES

A **grammar analogy** compares two sets of words. Each set is a pair of words that relate to each other in a grammatical way.
Example: hole : whole : : sea : see. *Hole* and *whole* are homophones just like *sea* and *see*.

Write the word that best completes each analogy.

1. _____ : happier : : clean : cleaner

2. anti : antidote : : _____ : predict

3. eat : _____ : : drink : drank

4. witch : _____ : : one : won

5. sleep : _____ : : run : ran

6. me : you : : mine : _____

7. child : _____ : : duck : ducks

8. _____ : ox : : geese : goose

9. _____ : cellar : : pedal : peddle

10. smart : _____ : : funny : funniest

11. mouse : _____ : : horse : horses

12. taller : tall : : _____ : bright

13. re : retreat : : _____ : submarine

14. he : _____ : : male : female

15. choose : chews : : _____ : paws

Write three of your own grammar analogies.

1. _____ : _____ : : _____ : _____

2. _____ : _____ : : _____ : _____

3. _____ : _____ : : _____ : _____

Reading Skills 3–4 • © 2004 Creative Teaching Press

Mixed Analogies Word Search

ANALOGIES

Fill in the missing word to complete each analogy. Then circle the words in the word search. (Hint: The first letter is provided for you.)

1. hot : cold : : l __ __ __ : right
2. dark : n __ __ __ __ : : sunny : daytime
3. m __ __ __ __ : coins : : glass : windows
4. coffee : cup : : s __ __ __ : bowl
5. hat : h __ __ __ : : shoes : feet
6. bird : f __ __ __ __ : : snake : slithers

7. hair : p __ __ __ __ __ : : fur : animals
8. stop : go : : r __ __ : green
9. boat : water : : p __ __ __ __ : air
10. city : c __ __ __ __ __ __ : : state : country
11. cow : farm : : b __ __ __ : forest
12. den : lion : : s __ __ : pig

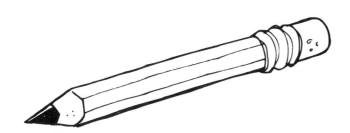

G	T	E	N	I	C	I	D	E	M	C	X	B
R	A	E	B	R	V	E	L	P	O	E	P	W
S	P	H	U	R	K	S	W	O	O	D	R	S
Y	N	X	A	E	T	I	S	Y	P	K	I	O
T	F	P	B	D	U	F	L	E	F	T	Q	U
N	T	L	E	C	A	A	G	J	M	H	C	P
U	L	A	I	D	T	F	H	W	E	G	R	D
O	O	N	E	E	P	F	S	A	N	I	D	Y
C	I	E	M	E	S	M	D	G	H	N	K	T
M	O	T	A	D	P	O	L	E	B	Z	A	S

Get in Shape with Analogies

ANALOGIES

This activity includes different types of analogies. Fill in the missing word to complete each analogy. The shapes of the letters are indicated with the boxes to help you.

1 pear : fruit : : artichoke

2 water : : : wood : solid

3 mustache : lip : : beard :

4 tires : cars : : : ice skates

5 papers : file : : clothes :

6 : winter : : hot : summer

7 days : : : months : year

8 scientist : lab : : teacher :

9 bud : : : puppy : dog

10 their : there : : hear :

Reading Skills 3–4 • © 2004 Creative Teaching Press

Name _____ Date _____

What's in a Name?

VOCABULARY

Read the clues. Determine which would be the best name for each situation based on the vocabulary choices. Explain why your choice makes sense. You may use a dictionary for help if needed.

There is a new Internet provider service on the market. It promises to deliver the fastest Internet connection possible. In fact, it claims to be ten times faster than anything available right now. Which name is the best?	
Expeditious Internet or **Progressive Internet**	Why?
There is a new movie being released next summer. It is a comedy. What is the best title?	
Humorous High Jinks or **Ridiculous Replays**	Why?
There is a new photocopy machine that says it can print posters in realistic color of anything you make on your computer. What is the best name for the machine?	
Multicolor 4000 or **Inky 4000**	Why?
Your friend just got a new dog and gave you the job of naming him. What is the best name for a calm, friendly pup?	
Spry or **Serenity**	Why?
You are going on vacation. There are only two hotels available. Which would be best for a restful stay?	
Uproarious Inn or **Tranquility Hotel**	Why?
There is a new video game about to hit the toy stores. The company just can't decide on a name that lets the buyer know that it is safe for kids. They claim it will make kids smarter. Which do you think is the best name?	
Insignificant Games or **Wise Ones**	Why?

Name _____ Date _____

Dictionary Damage

VOCABULARY

The definitions on this page are from a dictionary. However, the definitions are "damaged." Use a word from the word box to complete each definition.

addition	device	money	children
machine	liquid	take	bones
division	main	topic	life

1 **school**—a place for the instruction of _____ in different subjects

2 **compass**—a _____ used to track direction

3 **sum**—the answer to an _____ problem

4 **skeleton**—the _____ that frame a body

5 **evaporation**—the stage of the water cycle when a _____ turns into a gas

6 **budget**—the amount of _____ a person spends and how it will be spent

7 **paragraph**—a section of writing that includes a _____ sentence and a concluding sentence

8 **autobiography**—a book written by a person about his or her own

_____

9 **quotient**—the answer to a _____ problem

10 **summary**—the _____ points of a story

11 **seize**—to grasp or _____ something; to get possession

12 **manufacture**—to make something by hand or by _____ that can be sold

Reading Skills 3–4 • © 2004 Creative Teaching Press

Words in Words

Vocabulary

Look at the set of letters. Use them to make as many words as you can. Write the words in the matching box. Then try to identify the mystery word that can be spelled using all of the letters.

n	c	o	d	t	e	a	u	i

3-Letter Words

4-Letter Words

5-Letter Words

More Than 5-Letters

The secret word is _____.
(Hint: It is what you need to succeed.)

Name _____ Date _____

Newsworthy Vocabulary

VOCABULARY

Below are sections from a newspaper. Decide which section of the newspaper the vocabulary words would most likely be found. Write the words in that section.

president	elections	touchdown	thunderstorms	companies
soccer	stocks	plays	radar	theater
comics	movies	barometer	agreement	treaty
cloudy	television	budget	finals	banks

News

Sports

Weather

Entertainment

Money

Name _____ Date _____

Reading Materials Match-Up

VOCABULARY

Read each word in the right column. Then read each definition in the left column. Write the letter of the word that matches each definition.

Definitions

1 ____ a book that was written to teach you something; a factual book

2 ____ a fictional book that usually involves magic

3 ____ a story that is based on a famous person, location, or event from history

4 ____ something that may or may not rhyme, but usually has a rhythm when read

5 ____ a story that usually involves a hero

6 ____ a story that includes characters that do things that would never be possible in real life

7 ____ a story that is mostly based on facts, but has some elements of fiction for the plot

8 ____ a fictional story

9 ____ a story that is meant to teach a lesson

10 ____ a story that is fiction, but uses some factual scientific information which may be exaggerated

Words

a. legend

b. fairy tale

c. fable

d. poem

e. narrative story

f. nonfiction

g. fantasy

h. science fiction

i. historical fiction

j. realistic fiction

Comprehension

VOCABULARY

Use the words from the box to identify the parts of reading comprehension.

> inference   compare   vocabulary   sequence
> strategies   retell   opinion   contrast

1 This is the collection of words that you know, recognize, can explain, and understand when you are reading. _____

2 Some examples of these include rereading, using context clues, adjusting your rate when reading, and using picture clues to understand text.

_____

3 This is the order of the events. _____

4 This is what you should be able to do with all of the main ideas when you finish the story so someone else will know what the story was about.

_____

5 This is what you make when you think about what you know and add the clues given in the reading to assume something about the story.

_____

6 This is what you make when you say what you think about a story. It may be different than what another person thinks. _____

7 This is what you do when you think about how things are similar.

_____

8 This is what you do when you think about how things are different.

_____

Name _____ Date _____

Why?

QUESTION COMPREHENSION

You will often be asked to answer questions about what you read. It is important to know the different types of questions and how to respond to them. The "Why?" questions require thinking. They usually cannot be answered directly from what was read.

Answer the "thinking questions" that begin with "Why". Write your explanation in complete sentences, rewording the questions. The first one is started for you.

1 Why do people have eyelashes? _People have eyelashes because_ _____

_____

_____

2 Why do lifeguards sit so high up from the pool? _____

_____

_____

3 Why are coins different sizes? _____

_____

_____

4 Why do children go to school five out of seven days a week? _____

_____

_____

5 Why do cities have so much pollution? _____

_____

_____

6 Why do students have homework? _____

_____

_____

Name _____ Date _____

How?

QUESTION COMPREHENSION

You will often be asked to answer questions about what you read. It's important to know the different types of questions and how to respond to them. The "How?" questions require thinking. They usually ask you to tell the process of something.

Answer the "thinking questions" that begin with "How". Write your explanation in complete sentences, rewording the questions.

1 How does an e-mail get from one computer to another?

_____

_____

2 How does the mail carrier get the mail to your mailbox?

_____

_____

3 How does someone get elected into an office?

_____

_____

4 How do you make an ice-cream sandwich?

_____

_____

5 How does someone study for a test?

_____

_____

6 How does the sky get dark at night?

_____

_____

Reading Skills 3–4 • © 2004 Creative Teaching Press

Name _____ Date _____

Your Book or Your Head?

Question Comprehension

You will often be asked to answer questions about what you read. It is important to know the different types of questions and how to respond to them. "In the Book" questions are direct questions that have the answers right in the book. They usually begin with *who, what, when,* and *where.* "In Your Head" questions are thinking questions that require you to use what you read along with other information you know to answer the question. They usually begin with *how* or *why.*

Read each question. Decide whether it is an "In the Book" or "In Your Head question." Circle the book for "In the Book" or the head for "In Your Head."

1. Who was the first explorer to land in America?

2. How would a scientist plan a mission to Mercury?

3. Where were blue jeans invented?

4. Why did the author choose the forest for the setting?

5. How did the early missions get established?

6. When did the first airplane take off?

7. What caused the volcano to explode?

8. Why did the main character risk her life so many times?

9. What was the first thing that happened in this chapter?

10. How are you similar to the main character?

11. Why was the main character so confused?

12. When did the character solve the problem?

Name _____ Date _____

Some or All?

QUESTION COMPREHENSION

Watch out for questions that have the word *some* or *all*. They require you to measure the degree of fact in the question. For the answer to be *all* the statement must be a fact in EVERY case, without any exceptions.

Read each statement. Decide whether it is a fact. Bubble in either **True** or **False**.

True   **False**

1 ○ ○ All dentists are gentle.

2 ○ ○ Some dogs have tails.

3 ○ ○ Some pencils have erasers.

4 ○ ○ All movies make people laugh.

5 ○ ○ Some airplanes have wings.

6 ○ ○ All teeth have enamel.

7 ○ ○ All cities have subways.

8 ○ ○ Some people enjoy vacations.

9 ○ ○ Some classrooms are quiet.

10 ○ ○ All people have middle names.

11 ○ ○ All computers have a mouse.

12 ○ ○ All maps have continents.

13 ○ ○ All maps should have legends or keys.

14 ○ ○ Some people love math.

15 ○ ○ Some streets have traffic lights.

Name _____ Date _____

Indoor Smores

COMPREHENDING DIRECTIONS

Read the recipe for making Indoor Smores.

Indoor Smores

Coat a 9 x 13 inch baking dish with cooking spray. Pour 4
cups of honey graham cereal into a mixing bowl. Set
aside. Melt 3 tablespoons of margarine in a medium
saucepan over low heat. Slowly pour in 6 cups of mini-
marshmallows and 1/4 cup of light corn syrup. Mix slowly
in the pan until melted and smooth. Stir in 1 and 1/2 cups
of chocolate chips until they melt. Remove from heat and
pour over the cereal in the mixing bowl. Stir well until
all mixed together. Press into coated baking dish.
Cool completely. Cut into 16 squares. Serve.

Answer the questions.

1 What gets mixed in with the margarine while on the stove?

_____

2 When do you know you have stirred the chocolate chips long enough?

_____

3 How many people could enjoy the smores? _____

4 How many marshmallows do you need? _____

5 Why does the baking dish need to be coated?

_____

6 What do you need to do just before cutting and serving the smores?

_____

Sturdy Windsock

COMPREHENDING DIRECTIONS

Read the directions for making an unusual and sturdy windsock.

Get a 12 x 18 inch piece of craft foam. Use a hot glue gun or wood glue to attach smaller shapes of craft foam to form flowers. Layer the shapes for multicolored flowers. Let the glue dry. Roll the full piece of craft foam to form a tube. Staple the ends together. Punch two holes at the top of the tube. Tie on a small piece of yarn for a handle. Punch four to eight holes around the bottom of the tube. String a piece of yarn or raffia (1 yard long each) from each punched hole. Hang the windsock outside on a windy day.

Answer the questions.

1 What do you do after you decorate the full-sized piece of craft foam?

_____

2 What materials do you need to make this project?

_____

3 Why do the pieces of yarn or raffia need to be so long?

_____

4 What will this craft do?

_____

5 Why does it require wood glue or a hot glue gun instead of school glue?

_____

6 Why is it called a "sturdy" windsock?

_____

Reading Skills 3–4 • © 2004 Creative Teaching Press

Name _____ Date _____

Multiplication Race

COMPREHENDING DIRECTIONS

Read the directions for making this fun game.

For two players: Get a piece of 12 x 18 inch
construction paper. Draw 2-inch squares along the
perimeter of the paper. Label one square *start* and the
one to the right of that *finish*. Players move in a
clockwise direction. Get two dice and two markers. Roll
the dice. The person who rolls an even number goes
first. Roll two dice. Multiply the numbers together.
Move that number of spaces on the game board. The
first person to the finish line wins the game.

Answer the questions.

1 How is this game educational?

_____

_____

2 How many players can play the game? _____

3 How does a player move around the game board?

_____

_____

4 Who goes first?

_____

5 What other ways could the same materials be used to make a new game?

_____

_____

Mint Ice Cream

COMPREHENDING DIRECTIONS

Read the recipe for making this tasty treat.

Desserts

Get a 1-pound coffee can and a 3-pound coffee can. Place the 1-pound can in the middle of the 3-pound can. Fill the 1-pound can with 2 cups of whipping cream, 1/2 cup sugar, 1/2 teaspoon vanilla, 1/2 teaspoon peppermint, and several chopped-up peppermint sticks (or peppermint candy). Layer crushed ice and rock salt between the two cans. Put plastic lids on both cans. Sit on the floor with a friend. Roll the larger can back and forth for about 15 minutes. Remove the lids. Mix the ingredients with a wooden spoon. Serve.

Answer the questions.

1 Why do you need to roll the can for 15 minutes?

_____

2 What do you think are the most important ingredients for the flavor?

_____

3 Which ingredients help freeze the mixture?

_____

4 Why do you think the crushed ice and rock salt are outside the ice-cream can?

_____

5 What could you do if you wanted to make twice as much?

_____

Reading Skills 3–4 • © 2004 Creative Teaching Press

Name _____ Date _____

Follow That Recipe

Comprehending Directions

Read the recipe and answer the questions.

Ice Cream

Ingredients
1/2 cup milk   ice
1 tablespoon sugar   6 tablespoons salt
3/4 tablespoon vanilla

1. Put the milk, sugar, and vanilla in a small resealable plastic bag, and seal the bag.
2. Fill a large freezer bag half full of ice.
3. Add the salt to the ice.
4. Put the small bag inside the large bag, and seal the large bag.
5. Shake the bag for 5 minutes.
6. Put the bag in the freezer for a few minutes. The liquid will thicken like ice cream.

Answer the questions.

1 How many bags do you need to make this recipe? _____

2 What three ingredients are placed in the small plastic bag? _____

_____

3 How long do you need to shake the bag? _____

4 Number the steps in the correct order.

_____ Put the bag in the freezer.   _____ Put ice in a large freezer bag.

_____ Put the small bag in large bag.   _____ Put milk, sugar, and vanilla in

_____ Shake the bag.   small plastic bag.

_____ Add salt to the ice.

5 How many tablespoons of vanilla do you need? _____

Sort It Out

Categorization

Categorization is the ability to sort items into groups. It is a prerequisite skill for being able to identify the main idea and details of a story.

Sort the words into the correct baskets. Label each laundry basket with the category name. This will show the main idea and details of the group of words. The first basket is labeled for you.

sock	wind	red	muff
mist	leg	chill	magenta
hat	lung	neck	fog
tan	rib	turquoise	ring

Things you wear

Name _____ Date _____

Book Categories

CATEGORIZATION

Read the title of each book. Write what kind of book it is.

 Mystery Famous People Science  Sports Instructional Guide  Humor

1 Living Legends: The Story of Ten Rock Stars _____

2 Riddle Me with Riddles _____

3 The Case of the Broken Window _____

4 Everything You Need to Know About Ballet _____

5 Great Basketball Moments _____

6 The Joke's on You! _____

7 Unsolved Occurrences _____

8 Orbiting in Space _____

9 Snowboarding Fun _____

10 How to Build a Birdhouse _____

11 The Life of John F. Kennedy _____

12 Rocks, Minerals, and More _____

Name _____ Date _____

Sort the Words

Categorization

Write each item under the correct category.

Asia	letter	Texas	prairie	essay
magazine	Africa	desert	thunder	hail
tundra	helmet	Australia	jersey	sleet
Florida	Europe	sneakers	fog	New York
ocean	brochure	coat	Ohio	diary

States

_____

_____

_____

_____

Continents

_____

_____

_____

_____

Things to Wear

_____

_____

_____

_____

Things to Read

_____

_____

_____

_____

Weather

_____

_____

_____

_____

Habitats

_____

_____

_____

_____

Reading Skills 3–4 • © 2004 Creative Teaching Press

Odd One Out

CATEGORIZATION

Elimination is when one item doesn't belong in the same category with the others.

Read each group of words. Cross out the word that doesn't belong in the same category as the others. Then explain why it doesn't belong.

1 Iroquois Cherokee Shawnee Georgian _____

2 circle rectangle number diamond _____

3 history classroom math science _____

4 sheet pants socks dress _____

5 pond lake river country _____

6 continent valley mountain moon _____

7 lasagna doughnut cake eclair _____

8 pan sofa skillet pot _____

9 handsome attractive man charming _____

10 alert awake prepared late _____

11 north south west legend _____

12 bustle noise commotion friendly _____

13 carrot hay apples fish _____

14 quarter nickel dime penny _____

15 Africa America Australia Antarctica _____

Balanced Thinking

CATEGORIZATION

Read each group of words. Add one more item to the balance scale so the ideas balance.

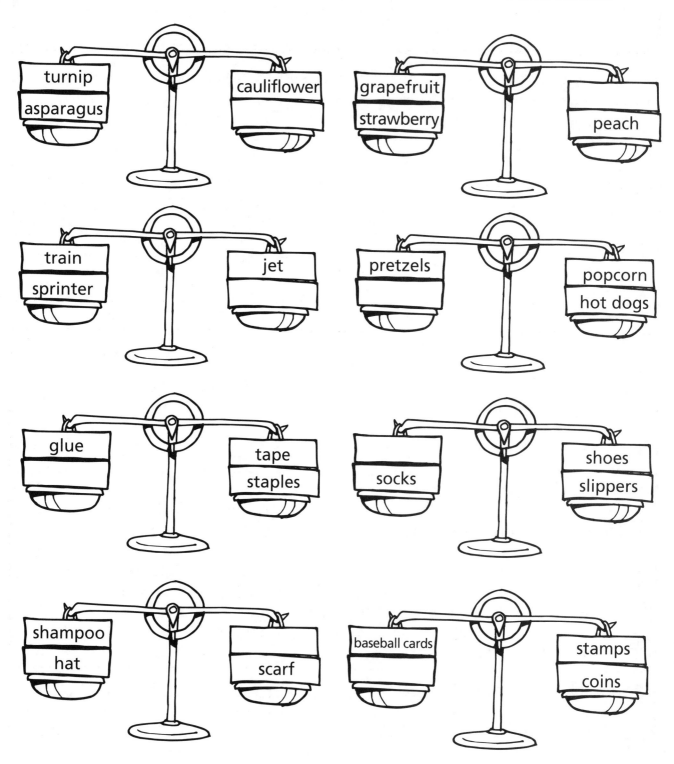

Reading Skills 3–4 • © 2004 Creative Teaching Press

Name _____ Date _____

TV Time

MAIN IDEA

The **main idea** of a story is the big picture. To find the main idea, think of all the details. The category that the details all fit into is the main idea.

Television stations often have a main idea of what type of shows they want to broadcast. In fact, many cable stations are named after the shows they choose to air. Read the titles of the shows that air on the television stations. Write each TV station on the menu guide.

Animal Network   Cartoon Channel   The Classics   The History Station   Fashion Fun   Game Shows   Technology Today   Cooking Channel

Station	8:00 p.m.	8:30 p.m.	9:00 p.m.
❶	War of 1812	American Revolution	Civil War Photos
❷	Wild Creatures	Monkey Movements	Jane Goodall
❸	Cartoon Capers	Classic Cartoons	Cartoon Junction
❹	Cheap Wardrobe II	Classic Clothes	Shoes, Shoes, Shoes
❺	Movies from 1950	Movies for the Early Years	Black and White Movies
❻	Password Gametime	Classic Games	Spell That Word!
❼	Microwave Mania	Kid-Tested Treats	Delicious Desserts
❽	Gadgets Galore	Electronics Exhibition	Computer Capers

Name _____ Date _____

Main Idea Tree Diagram

Main Idea

Read each detail in the tree diagram. Fill in the main idea (the big picture) that comes to mind after reading all of the details.

```
┌─────────────────┐        ┌──────────────────────────────────────────┐
│                 │        │ Goldilocks walked through the forest alone.│
│                 │        └──────────────────────────────────────────┘
│                 │        ┌──────────────────────────────────────────┐
│                 │        │ Goldilocks entered a stranger's home.      │
│                 │        └──────────────────────────────────────────┘
│                 │        ┌──────────────────────────────────────────┐
│                 │        │ Goldilocks slept in a bed and ate food from│
│                 │        │ a stranger's home.                         │
└─────────────────┘        └──────────────────────────────────────────┘
```

```
┌─────────────────┐        ┌──────────────────────────────────────────┐
│                 │        │ Positive comments make people feel better  │
│                 │        │ about themselves.                          │
│                 │        └──────────────────────────────────────────┘
│                 │        ┌──────────────────────────────────────────┐
│                 │        │ People smile at those who smile at them.   │
│                 │        └──────────────────────────────────────────┘
│                 │        ┌──────────────────────────────────────────┐
│                 │        │ People feel better when they smile.        │
└─────────────────┘        └──────────────────────────────────────────┘
```

```
┌─────────────────┐        ┌──────────────────────────────────────────┐
│                 │        │ Some people do the same things every day   │
│                 │        │ in the exact same order.                   │
│                 │        └──────────────────────────────────────────┘
│                 │        ┌──────────────────────────────────────────┐
│                 │        │ Some people eat at the same restaurants    │
│                 │        │ over and over again.                       │
│                 │        └──────────────────────────────────────────┘
│                 │        ┌──────────────────────────────────────────┐
│                 │        │ Some people don't like to do anything they │
│                 │        │ haven't done before.                       │
└─────────────────┘        └──────────────────────────────────────────┘
```

Reading Skills 3–4 • © 2004 Creative Teaching Press

What's the Topic?

Main Idea

Read each short paragraph. Write the main idea at the top of each paragraph.

① Main Topic:

Pluto is the farthest planet from the Sun. Since it is approximately 3.6 billion miles away from the Sun, the temperature is -369 degrees Fahrenheit. The surface of the planet is made up of rock with gases. Due to its distance from the Sun, it is unlikely that anyone will ever travel to the planet.

② Main Topic:

Of the many types of music, country music seems to go in and out of popularity. Country music is based on southern mountain music. In the 1920s there was a radio show called the Grand Ole Opry in Nashville, Tennessee. Today, visitors go to the Grand Ole Opry to hear country music concerts.

③ Main Topic:

Anything that anyone dumps on the ground or down the drain finds its way into the water cycle. This often leads to polluted water. Polluted water can't be used for watering crops, drinking, or swimming. In fact, it is unhealthy and often dangerous to all life forms. The major sources of pollution include sewage, chemicals from factories, fertilizers, weed killers, and leaking landfills. It is estimated that around the world, five million people die each year from illnesses caused by polluted water that got into the water cycle.

④ Main Topic:

Sir Isaac Newton was a British scientist famous for many important discoveries that affect our lives today. It is thanks to him that we now understand how gravity holds things down on Earth. He also showed how sunlight is made up of all the colors of the rainbow. During his life (1642–1727), he made many important discoveries in the areas of math and science.

Name _____ Date _____

Headlines

Main Idea

The headlines of newspaper articles often tell the reader the main idea of the article. Read the newspaper articles. Choose the best headline for each article.

1 The storm was even more powerful than predicted. Many homes on the sand were completely destroyed. The hundreds of sandbags that were set up to keep the homes safe were useless. Luckily, the people who lived in the beachfront homes left just in time. Everyone escaped the dangerous wind and waves safely.

Safe from the Storm, The Destructive Storm, Beach Homes in Danger

2 In fact, studies have shown that children who have pets are happier and more patient than children without pets. The children who were a part of the study said that they would talk to their pets when they had problems or worries. The researchers discovered that when the children talked to their pets their heart rate went down and they were more calm and relaxed.

Pets Help People, Buy More Pets, Pet Science

3 What an upset! The local basketball team hasn't won a game in three months. Last night, they played the third place team in the league and won. Due to their poor record, attendance has been down for the past month. Only four hundred people were at the game in support of the struggling team. Those four hundred people had one exciting night!

Another Loss, Attendance Is Down, Beating the Odds

Reading Skills 3–4 • © 2004 Creative Teaching Press

The Main Idea

MAIN IDEA

Write the main idea for each list of details.

1 I see the red, orange, yellow, green, and blue arches of color.
It gleamed in the sky after a rainy day.
It is such a beautiful sight.

_____

2 We traveled to South America to visit this wondrous place.
Everything is green and plush because of the abundance of rainfall.
It is the home to many plants and animals.

_____

3 I saw several different animals there.
Some of the animals live in cages. Others live in an outdoor space that is set
up to look and feel like the animal's natural habitat.
There are several exhibits and shows to see throughout the day.

_____

4 There are several things I do each week. I help my father with the gardening.
I take out the trash and help set the table.
I clean my room and put all my clothes away.

_____

5 The main ingredients are cheese, tomato sauce, and a crust.
There are several other items that can be placed on top: pepperoni,
mushrooms, sausage, bell peppers, onions, and olives.
It's my favorite thing to eat for lunch.

_____

6 I enjoy spending time with Tonya.
We talk on the phone every day and discuss a variety of topics.
We have several things in common. We both like to ice skate, shop, and read
books.

_____

Comic Capers

PREDICTING

> **Predicting** is the ability to guess what will happen before it occurs. It requires you to think about what you already know, what makes sense, and the story itself. Predictions may change as you read. People make different predictions based on their background knowledge.

Read the comics. Predict what will happen next. Write your predicition on the line.

1 Prediction _____

_____

2 Prediction _____

_____

3 Prediction _____

_____

Reading Skills 3–4 • © 2004 Creative Teaching Press

Name _____ Date _____

Picture Prediction

PREDICTING

Look at each book cover. Read the three titles. Circle the title that descibes what the book is probably about.

  The Princess Parade
Barbara's Pet
Zoo Clues

  Technology Tricks
Literary Greats
TV and Telephones

  Baseball Greats
How to Play Football
Indoor Games

  Sally's Stables
The Berry Bunch
Me and Midge

  Computer Skills
Delicious Dinner
Dishes
Candy Treats

  Grand Games
The Case of the
    Missing Teacher
Riddles, Riddles,
    Riddles

Predict a Book

PREDICTING

Read each book title. Predict what the book will be about based on its title. Write one complete sentence about your prediction.

1 The Spooky Chronicles _____
_____

2 Mission to Mercury _____
_____

3 Batty Flight _____
_____

4 The Super Savers Scrapbook _____
_____

5 Break the Bank _____
_____

6 Funny Females of the Forties _____
_____

7 Movie Mayhem _____
_____

8 Organized Living _____
_____

9 Awesome Eruptions _____
_____

10 Party Time _____
_____

11 Vacation Vibes _____
_____

12 Arachnophobia _____
_____

Reading Skills 3–4 • © 2004 Creative Teaching Press

Name _____ Date _____

What Is That Web Site?

Look at the names of the imaginary Web sites. Predict what you could most likely do on each Web site. Write your prediction on the computer screen.

1
www.withapaintbrush.com

4
www.moneymanianow.com

7
www.subscriberightnow.com

2
www.sofasright2u.com

5
www.cartoonsrightnow.com

8
www.jobsatyourfingertips.com

3
www.logic4kids.com

6
www.howsthehomeworkgoing.com

9
www.videogames2go.com

Name _____ Date _____

What Will Happen?

Predicting

Read each event. Write a prediction about what will happen next.

1 A student came to class without his homework.

_____

2 Gas prices are going up and Mr. Rish has a big truck.

_____

3 Ms. Smith got a flat tire on her way to work.

_____

4 The cat started to meow in the middle of the night.

_____

5 The head of the company was caught spending too much money.

_____

6 A toy store has just announced a "Going Out of Business" Sale.

_____

7 Everyone wants the new Talking Toto toy for their youngsters.

_____

8 The price of DVD recorders is going down.

_____

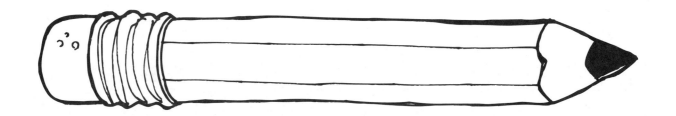

Reading Skills 3–4 • © 2004 Creative Teaching Press

Name _____ Date _____

Good or Evil?

STORY ELEMENTS: CHARACTERS

In most fiction books, the author includes at least two kinds of characters—antagonist and protagonist.
    Protagonist—the person the reader is rooting for.
    Antagonist—the person the reader is rooting against.

Read the each description of a character from a book. Fill in the circle next to 👍 if the character is a protagonist (good) or next to 👎 if the character is an antagonist (bad).

1 ○ 👍 ○ 👎 He tries to trick the other characters into doing what he wants, even if they get hurt.

2 ○ 👍 ○ 👎 She tries to make a poisoned pudding.

3 ○ 👍 ○ 👎 She helps the little bird get better and then sets it free.

4 ○ 👍 ○ 👎 The hungry lion tries to talk the squirrel into coming to his den.

5 ○ 👍 ○ 👎 He sells the woman's house to make money while she ends up without a home.

6 ○ 👍 ○ 👎 She offers to help all of the other characters.

7 ○ 👍 ○ 👎 She is patient, trustworthy, and generous.

8 ○ 👍 ○ 👎 She is selfish, sneaky, and rude.

9 ○ 👍 ○ 👎 He lies to the other characters.

10 ○ 👍 ○ 👎 He cheats the hermit crab out of its only shell.

11 ○ 👍 ○ 👎 She lights a fire in a national forest.

12 ○ 👍 ○ 👎 He helps blind people learn how to read Braille.

13 ○ 👍 ○ 👎 He offers to fly the main character to safety.

14 ○ 👍 ○ 👎 She gives up her last can of soup to help another character.

15 ○ 👍 ○ 👎 She spends all of her time spinning webs to help the main character.

Reading Skills 3-4 • © 2004 Creative Teaching Press

Name _____ Date _____

What a Character!

STORY ELEMENTS: CHARACTERS

Read the clues about some very famous characters in literature. The authors did such a great job of painting the image of the character that you can immediately recognize the characters from the descriptions if you've read or heard the story before. Write the characters below the clues.

Charlie	Baby Bear	Wolf	Giant
Cinderella	Hare	Pinocchio	Humpty Dumpty

1 I was a very kind, patient, and thoughtful boy. I lived with my loving parents and grandparents. We were very poor, so I tried to save my money. One day, I won a visit to a candy factory. The other characters didn't deserve to be there. I appreciated my visit. My honesty paid off. Who am I?

_____

2 I am young and friendly. I was sad to find my breakfast eaten after returning home from a walk. I found a little girl in my bed. I wanted to be her friend, but she ran off. Who am I?

_____

3 I ran in a race. I always teased the turtle by telling him he was so slow. I was a bit lazy when I stopped to take a nap. I was sure I would win the race anyway. I was shocked when I found out the turtle beat me! Who am I?

_____

4 I followed a little girl as she was walking to her grandma's house. I was very hungry. I tricked her many times. I am a sneaky character who will do anything to get what I want. Who am I?

_____

5 I was a nice little girl who was treated very badly by my family. I was patient and obeyed every order they gave me. I worked very hard, doing all of the work for my two stepsisters. Luckily, my kindness was soon rewarded by some strange events. Who am I?

_____

6 I was lucky to be a little boy, but I had a bad habit of lying. I always got caught since you could truly see the lies on my face. I'm not sure if I ever learned my lesson. Who am I?

_____

7 I lived above the clouds. A little boy climbed up to my home. I was very angry to see him at first. He stole my goose. Who am I?

_____

8 I was foolish. I didn't listen to everyone's advice not to climb up high walls. I should have followed directions and respected others better. I fell off the wall. People tried to help me, but it was too late. Who am I?

_____

Get Set

STORY ELEMENTS: SETTING

Read the characteristics of each setting. Write the first place that comes to your mind. Draw a picture of what that setting would look like.

Characteristics of Location	Setting	What I Picture
• swings • slide • sand • kids • bars • paths		
• snow • squirrels • trees • chains • blue jays • skis		
• lemurs • rain • trees • sloth • insects • plants		
• flowers • lava • ash • green • mountain • red		

Name _____ Date _____

Which Setting?

STORY ELEMENTS: SETTING

Some famous authors are writing books. They have some basic ideas about what they want their stories to be about. They just can't figure out the best setting, so they've asked for your help. Read each author's plan. Write the best setting for the story.

Main Characters	Plot	Settings	
		Time	Place
a mouse a rat a cat a farmer	The mouse and rat team up against the farmer for land space, but the cat is always in the way.	past present future	
2 fourth graders— boy and girl teacher custodian	Two friends discover a secret doorway to past events and lives. Many secrets are revealed.	past present future	
a ten-year-old girl and her brother	The children start a detective agency and solve mysteries in every chapter.	past present future	
10 spiders 5 snails 2 grasshoppers	The bugs gathered together to form a club with a mission to scare the people out of their house.	past present future	

Reading Skills 3–4 • © 2004 Creative Teaching Press

Name _____ Date _____

Parts of a Story Crossword

STORY ELEMENTS

Read each clue. Identify the part of a story (example: plot, setting, characters) that matches the clue. Use these words to complete the crossword puzzle.

Across

1. These are the people or animals that are in the story.
4. This is the story line of what happens.
5. This is the person who saves the day.
7. This is where the story starts.
9. The opposite of the details. It gives you the big picture of the most important thing to remember.
10. This is when the story is over.
12. This is usually the bad character. (Hint: The first letter is "v.")

Down

2. This is where the story takes place.
3. These end the problems.
6. These need solutions.
8. This is the part of the story between the beginning and the end when the exciting parts usually happen.
11. These are the opposite of the main ideas. They help paint a clear picture in your mind.

Name _____ Date _____

The Basic Idea

SEQUENCING

Sequencing is the ability to put events in order so that they make sense in the story, follow a timeline, or retell a story in order.

Look at the set of words in each box. Number them from 1 to 4 to put them in a logical order.

a	**b**	**c**	**d**
_____ today	_____ April	_____ Spring	_____ dawn
_____ yesterday	_____ December	_____ Fall	_____ afternoon
_____ tomorrow	_____ May	_____ Winter	_____ midnight
_____ next week	_____ June	_____ Summer	_____ dusk

e	**f**	**g**	**h**
_____ water	_____ retirement	_____ Fifth St.	_____ mix
_____ plant	_____ birth	_____ Tenth St.	_____ pour
_____ trim	_____ working	_____ Second St.	_____ eat
_____ pick	_____ elementary school	_____ Ninth St.	_____ bake

Reading Skills 3–4 • © 2004 Creative Teaching Press

Order It

Sequencing

Read the steps for each activity. Number the steps from 1 to 5 to show the correct order.

Laundry Day

_____ Fold the clothes.

_____ Dry the clothes.

_____ Sort the clothes.

_____ Wash the clothes.

_____ Put the clothes in the laundry basket.

Making Hot Chocolate

_____ Enjoy with a peppermint stick.

_____ Stir until mixed together.

_____ Put chocolate in a cup.

_____ Put the cup in the microwave for three minutes.

_____ Add milk to the chocolate.

Sending a Letter

_____ Get an envelope.

_____ Put the envelope in the mailbox.

_____ Put the letter in the envelope.

_____ Write the letter.

_____ Put a stamp on the envelope.

Going to Bed

_____ Climb under the covers.

_____ Fall asleep.

_____ Put on your pajamas.

_____ Turn off the light.

_____ Fix the blankets.

Name _____ Date _____

In What Order?

SEQUENCING

Read the title of each book. Number the events of the story line (plot) to show a logical order.

The Picnic in the Park

____ The friends eat a sandwich.

____ The responsible friends throw away the trash.

____ The friends drive to the park.

____ They set up the picnic blanket.

____ They drive home from the park very tired.

____ They enjoy playing on the swings and slides.

The Television Studio

____ They watched the taping of the show.

____ The host said that the 16th caller would win tickets to the taping of Shellie's favorite TV show.

____ Shellie and Kim drove to the television studio.

____ Before leaving, they hugged their favorite star and received autographed pictures.

____ There was an announcement on the radio.

____ Shellie called the radio station and was the 16th caller.

____ It was possibly the best day of their lives.

Grandma's Cookies

____ Ashley got the milk out of the refrigerator.

____ Grandma and Ashley talked about her day at school while they ate cookies.

____ Ashley came home after school.

____ Her grandma offered her some freshly baked cookies.

____ Ashley thanked her grandma for baking her favorite cookies.

The Sleepover

____ Aaron was so proud of himself for spending the night away from home for the first time.

____ Aaron got his invitation to Josh's party.

____ Aaron's mom drove him over to Josh's house.

____ The boys fell asleep.

____ Aaron was nervous. He had never spent the night at a friend's house before.

____ It was Josh's birthday, and he made invitations to a sleepover party.

____ The boys watched a scary movie while eating buttery popcorn.

Reading Skills 3–4 • © 2004 Creative Teaching Press

Name _____ Date _____

Story Ordering

SEQUENCING

Sequencing means arranging things in a logical order. For a story, that order is often chronological, or time order.

Read each story idea and the details that follow it. Number the details in the proper sequence.

1 Megan meets a new neighbor and makes a friend.

____ A girl of about 12 came around the corner.

____ The girls discovered that they both loved soccer.

____ The moving van unloaded furniture next door.

____ Anna introduced herself to Megan.

____ Megan noticed a girl's bike on the lawn.

2 Ryan's parents surprise him with the puppy that he's always wanted.

____ They placed the puppy in a basket with a large bow.

____ Ryan's parents finally decided to get him the dog.

____ Ryan was thrilled when he saw his new friend!

____ They picked out a ten-week-old puppy.

____ Ryan has been asking his parents for a puppy since he was 5 years old.

3 Ms. Webster's class puts on a play.

____ Ms. Webster posted the roles and behind-the-scenes jobs.

____ Ms. Webster suggested that the class put on a play.

____ After weeks of rehearsal, the performance was a success.

____ The class read many plays before selecting the perfect one.

____ Students signed up for the role or job they wanted.

Reading Skills 3–4 • © 2004 Creative Teaching Press

Name _____ Date _____

Note Card Nightmare

SEQUENCING

Mike dropped the note cards he had prepared for his speech "My Life Story." Order the cards by writing the correct number in each box.

My dad coached my 5th grade baseball team. We won the championship.

I began taking piano lessons at age 7.

I was born early in the morning on Thanksgiving Day.

The summer after winning the baseball championship, my family went to the beach on vacation.

My favorite animal when I was a baby was a teddy bear that sang when you squeezed it.

My favorite teacher was my 7th grade English teacher.

My brother was born when I was 5.

I got braces and glasses in 6th grade.

Reading Skills 3–4 • © 2004 Creative Teaching Press

Name _____ Date _____

New Words

CONTEXT CLUES

Context clues help you figure out the meaning of words you don't know. They include the words around the unknown word, the main idea of the story, and what you already know.

Circle the word that best fits in each sentence. Use the context clues to help make your decision.

1 The navigator studied the _____ to figure out which direction he was going.

   map   compass   television

2 Some days she felt so lethargic that she just didn't want to _____.

   yell   move   help

3 There was a conflict on the playground in which two friends were _____, but a teacher intervened and it was settled.

   hugging   playing   arguing

4 When the teacher said there would be no homework, the students cheered uproariously, making far too much _____ in the classroom.

   noise   mess   crying

5 The girl was becoming frustrated, although she tried not to show it by getting _____ with herself.

   angry   messy   lonely

6 Using their incisors, beavers can cut through bark and _____ on logs as they build their homes.

   roll   play   nibble

Name _____ Date _____

Finish the Story

Context Clues

Read the story. Fill in the blanks with words from the word box that would make sense in the story.

genuine	neglected	ridiculous	believing
definitely	assisting	vibrating	ordinary
ancient	amazement	discovered	shiny

The Magic Coin

I know you will have a hard time _____ what I am about to tell you,
_____
                                                    1

but I promise it is the whole truth and nothing but the truth. It all started the

night after my birthday party. I was _____ my mom with the chores
                                                            2

just like any _____ day. Suddenly, I _____ that there was
                       3   4

something rattling in the bottom of one of my gift boxes. I was sure that I had

taken all of the gifts out of the boxes as I opened them. How could I have

_____ a gift? I shook the box again. There was _____
          5   6

something still in the box! I lifted up the tissue paper and found a large,

_____ gold coin. It looked _____, like it could have been three
       7   8

hundred years old! Since I had gotten chocolate coins before, I bit into it just to

make sure it was _____. To my _____, it wasn't chocolate. It
                          9   10

was a real gold coin! What a shock! I put it in my pocket for safe keeping. A few

hours later, the coin started moving around in my pocket. I jumped so high that I

dropped all of the wrapping paper. What in the world was happening? I took

the _____ coin out of my pocket. I know it seems like a _____
            11   12

thought, but I figured it was worth a shot. I made a wish and rubbed the coin!

You won't believe it! My wish came true!

Reading Skills 3–4 • © 2004 Creative Teaching Press

Name _____ Date _____

Figure It Out

CONTEXT CLUES

Read the paragraph. Then read it again. Use the context clues to figure out the meaning of the words in bold print. Remember to think about the main ideas and look at the surrounding words.

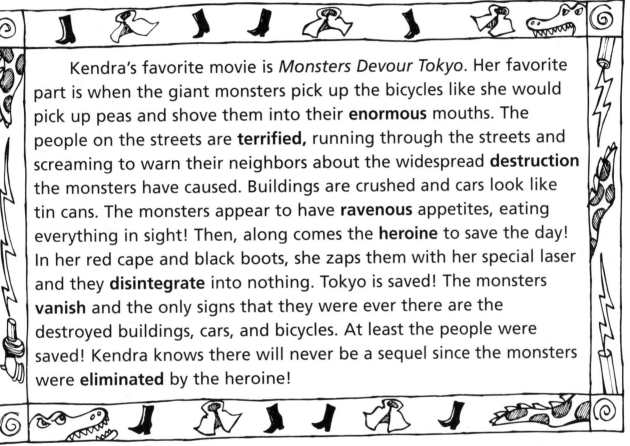

Kendra's favorite movie is *Monsters Devour Tokyo*. Her favorite part is when the giant monsters pick up the bicycles like she would pick up peas and shove them into their **enormous** mouths. The people on the streets are **terrified,** running through the streets and screaming to warn their neighbors about the widespread **destruction** the monsters have caused. Buildings are crushed and cars look like tin cans. The monsters appear to have **ravenous** appetites, eating everything in sight! Then, along comes the **heroine** to save the day! In her red cape and black boots, she zaps them with her special laser and they **disintegrate** into nothing. Tokyo is saved! The monsters **vanish** and the only signs that they were ever there are the destroyed buildings, cars, and bicycles. At least the people were saved! Kendra knows there will never be a sequel since the monsters were **eliminated** by the heroine!

Write the meaning of each word.

enormous _____

terrified _____

destruction _____

ravenous _____

heroine _____

disintegrate _____

vanish _____

eliminated _____

Name _____ Date _____

Context Clues Crossword

CONTEXT CLUES

Read each sentence. Look at the words in the word bank. Choose the word that makes the most sense in the sentence. Fill in the crossword puzzle.

control	decide	awkward	wanted	dispute
relax	complicated	fearless	bad	foolish
alone				

Across

1. The girl was very energetic. Her family had a hard time getting her to _____.
3. The man was _____ on his adventure. He couldn't wait to see the wild crocodiles.
4. He was in a state of confusion. He couldn't _____ what he should do.
5. She enjoyed her solitude. It was very peaceful when she was _____ under a tree.
7. The problem was impossible to solve. She thought it was too _____ for her class.

Down

2. It was an _____ situation. He felt embarrassed and didn't know what to say.
3. What a ridiculous way to spend money. He was _____ to waste it all on candy.
4. The teacher tried to settle the _____ so the children could be friends again.
6. The girl tried to persuade her mother to give her what she _____, but her mother said "no."
7. He felt like he lost all _____ of his people. He just couldn't govern or regulate anymore.
8. He dreaded the task. Just the thought of it gave him a _____ feeling in the pit of his stomach

Reading Skills 3–4 • © 2004 Creative Teaching Press

Name _____ Date _____

What Else Fits?

CONTEXT CLUES

Choose the correct word to replace the word in bold print in each sentence.

1 The campers paddled down the river in their **kayak.**
   a. bicycle   **c.** canoe
   b. car   **d.** tent

2 The hungry lion **devoured** all of its lunch.
   a. ate   **c.** cooked
   b. smelled   **d.** ran

3 The **greedy** girl did not share her candy with anyone else.
   a. generous   **c.** friendly
   b. selfish   **d.** happy

4 Trudy's team gave their best **effort** to win the game.
   a. time   **c.** lose
   b. shirt   **d.** try

5 The children went around and around on the **carousel** at the fair.
   a. swing   **c.** balloon
   b. bench   **d.** merry-go-round

6 Steve **devoted** a lot of time to finishing his science fair project.
   a. dedicated   **c.** hated
   b. wasted   **d.** liked

7 I could not have finished the job without her **assistance.**
   a. job   **c.** telephone
   b. help   **d.** laundry

8 I tried to **comprehend** all of the information so I could explain it to my brother.
   a. drive   **c.** understand
   b. discuss   **d.** file

Name _____ Date _____

Many Effects

CAUSE AND EFFECT

The **effect** is what happened. The **cause** is why it happened.

Fill in each graphic organizer by writing three effects (things that could happen) for each situation (cause).

Cause
You forgot to do your homework last night.

| Effect: |
| Effect: |
| Effect: |

Cause
You read a half hour every night.

| Effect: |
| Effect: |
| Effect: |

Cause
You stop watching television during the week.

| Effect: |
| Effect: |
| Effect: |

Cause
You decide to run for the student council.

| Effect: |
| Effect: |
| Effect: |

Cause
You make your bed every morning without being asked.

| Effect: |
| Effect: |
| Effect: |

Reading Skills 3–4 • © 2004 Creative Teaching Press

Name _____ Date _____

Many Possible Causes

CAUSE AND EFFECT

Fill in each graphic organizer by writing three causes (why something happens) for each outcome (effect).

| Cause: |
| Cause: |
| Cause: |

Effect
A boy puts on a pair of gloves.

| Cause: |
| Cause: |
| Cause: |

Effect
A woman calls for a tow truck.

| Cause: |
| Cause: |
| Cause: |

Effect
You hear an alarm go off.

| Cause: |
| Cause: |
| Cause: |

Effect
Water is running down the gutter.

| Cause: |
| Cause: |
| Cause: |

Effect
The dog is barking.

Reading Skills 3–4 • © 2004 Creative Teaching Press

Causes and Effects

CAUSE AND EFFECT

The **cause** is why it happened.   The **effect** is what happened.

Read each sentence. Underline the cause and circle the effect.

1. The children froze on the playground when they heard the bell ring.

2. Since the bill was late, she had to pay a fine.

3. They went down the waterslide to cool off on the hot summer day.

4. They threw the balloon away after it popped.

5. Before going on a walk, she put the leash on her dog.

6. She had a stomachache after eating too many pieces of candy.

7. He fell off his bike and cut his knee.

8. The television went off when the electricity went out.

9. The car stopped when it reached the red light.

10. When the movie let out, the people left the theater.

11. Glass was all over the floor after she dropped the picture frame.

12. He was pleased to see that he had lost five pounds by running on the treadmill daily for a week.

13. She was twitching in her sleep since she was dreaming.

14. He sneezed because he had bad allergies.

15. She bought a new toothbrush because hers was getting old.

Reading Skills 3–4 • © 2004 Creative Teaching Press

Name _____ Date _____

Match 'Em Up

CAUSE AND EFFECT

Below are causes and effects. Read each effect on the left. Write the letter of the most logical cause from the list on the right.

Effects

1 _____ he bought a smoothie

2 _____ she packed her suitcase

3 _____ he sharpened his pencil

4 _____ they packed up the tent

5 _____ the flashlight wasn't working

6 _____ he put on a tuxedo

7 _____ she bought a cradle

8 _____ he opened his umbrella

9 _____ she turned the page on the calendar

10 _____ she bought a map

Causes

a. it was time to go home

b. the batteries were dead

c. it started to rain

d. the wedding would begin in an hour

e. the trip would begin tomorrow

f. it was a new month

g. the baby would be born soon

h. it broke

i. to find the right directions to the museum

j. he was thirsty

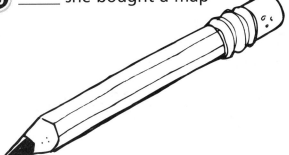

Write three sentences using any sets of matched phrases from above.

1 _____

2 _____

3 _____

If... Then

CAUSE AND EFFECT

Circle the letter of the choice that is NOT a likely effect of each statement.

1 If you do not eat breakfast—

   a. you will have a lot of energy.
   b. you will feel tired.
   c. you will be hungry.
   d. you may get sick.

2 If you do not cut your grass—

   a. your neighbors will be upset.
   b. your yard will look well maintained.
   c. weeds will grow tall.
   d. your house will look shabby.

3 If Marcus practices piano every day—

   a. he will be able to play songs well.
   b. he will perform well at his recital.
   c. he will feel proud.
   d. he will be unprepared.

4 If you forget to turn off the water in the bathroom—

   a. it will make a mess.
   b. it will flood the room.
   c. your mom will thank you.
   d. you will need to clean up.

5 If you do not return your library book—

   a. you may have a fine to pay.
   b. you might not be able to check out books.
   c. you will be rewarded for your actions.
   d. you may need to speak to the librarian.

6 If you work after school—

   a. you will have extra money.
   b. you will need to manage your time.
   c. you will learn new skills.
   d. you will be irresponsible.

Fact or Opinion?

FACT AND OPINION

A **fact** is a true statement that can be proven.
An **opinion** is a belief or feeling that cannot be proven. It may or may not be true.

Read each sentence. Decide whether it states a fact or an opinion. Write **F** if it is a fact or **O** if it is an opinion.

1 _____ The restaurant serves the best tortilla soup in the county.

2 _____ She has the friendliest dog.

3 _____ Mr. Arias is a teacher.

4 _____ The ice-cream shop opens at 9:30 a.m.

5 _____ The most popular vacation spot is Hawaii.

6 _____ Grapes grow on vines.

7 _____ Grocery stores sell the best meat.

8 _____ Every house should have a pool if the summer temperatures rise over

90 degrees.

9 _____ A passport is required to visit another country.

10 _____ Photocopy machines require ink.

11 _____ It is healthier to drink milk than juice.

12 _____ The book is science fiction.

13 _____ The reporter deserved the award.

14 _____ A family of owls lives in the branches of the tree by the library.

15 _____ All students know their multiplication tables.

Name _____ Date _____

Getting Personal

Fact and Opinion

Read each topic. Read the facts and opinions about the topic. Write two more facts and two more opinions.

Your School

It serves grades _____ to _____.

_____

_____

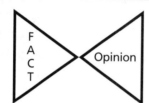

It is the best school in the state.

_____

_____

Your Favorite Resturant

It is called _____.

_____

_____

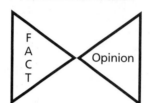

It makes the tastiest _____.

_____

_____

Your Favorite Book

The title is _____.

_____

_____

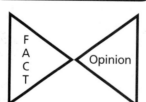

It is worthy of an award.

_____

_____

Your Favorite Animal

It is in the _____ family.

_____

_____

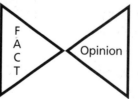

It is the most popular animal among children my age.

_____

_____

82

Name _____ Date _____

Unbelievable Ads

FACT AND OPINION

Read each advertisement. Underline all of the facts that could be proven. Circle all the opinions.

1 "Everybody loves the Yum! Yum! brand chocolate chip cookies. The stores sell out of them as soon as they arrive. In a blind taste test of one thousand children, one out of every two kids liked the Yum! Yum! brand over the other leading brand. Our chocolate chip cookies have chips that melt in your mouth. They are chewy and fit right in your hand. You can even microwave them to make them warm. Don't be left out! Hurry to your local store right away! Yum! Yum! brand chocolate chip cookies are the best tasting cookies you can buy!"

2 "Come on down to Crazy Cal's Computer Superstore today to save three hundred dollars on the new X515 computer system. It comes complete with the keyboard, monitor, and memory chips. We have 52 in stock ready to sell. The speed can't be beat! Everyone agrees that it is the best computer on the market. It deserves to win the Cool Computer Award at this year's Computer Expo. Kids around the world are adding it to their wish list. There are fifteen pre-installed games ready to be played. Hurry to Crazy Cal's Computer Superstore today to get the best computer ever created!"

Reading Skills 3–4 • © 2004 Creative Teaching Press

You Be the Judge

Fact and Opinion

Judge Julie has just heard the case of Fact Farley vs. Opinion Opie. She cannot judge the case because the court reporter who took the notes has mixed them all up. Help Judge Julie sort out the details of the case.

Write the number for each statement in the box under Fact Farley if the statement can be proven. If it cannot be proven, then write the number for that statement in the box under Opinion Opie. When you add up the value of the numbers in each person's box, you will know the winner of the case.

Fact Farley

Opinion Opie

Who Won the Case?

1 I am the most responsible person in the whole school.

2 I have a feeling that she took it.

3 My backpack was zipped.

4 Everyone knows that I always tell the truth.

5 My teacher thinks I'm the best student.

6 My backpack is green with a purple zipper.

7 The backpack was on the third hook.

8 The backpack has a pocket on the front.

9 I have the most organized desk.

10 The game was in the backpack.

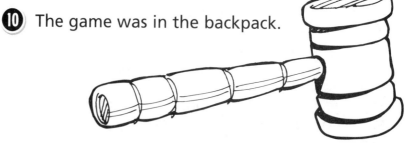

Reading Skills 3–4 • © 2004 Creative Teaching Press

Name _____ Date _____

TV Guide Budget

> A **summary** tells only the most important parts of what was read, seen, or heard. It includes only the most important main ideas.

Channel APAN is getting ready to publish its upcoming television shows in the television guide that is sent out in newspapers. The newspaper charges $ 0.10 per word. Channel APAN can only afford $2.00 per television show listing.

Write three summaries of television shows or movies that could be shown on Channel APAN. Remember to make sure each listing will cost $2.00 or less.

Title of show:	Length of show:
Summary: _____ _____ _____	
Cost of listing: $ _____	Within budget? yes no

Title of show:	Length of show:
Summary: _____ _____ _____	
Cost of listing: $ _____	Within budget? yes no

Title of show:	Length of show:
Summary: _____ _____ _____	
Cost of listing: $ _____	Within budget? yes no

Name _____ Date _____

Book Summary

SUMMARIZING

Read each book summary. Decide which title from the box matches each summary. Write the title on the line.

> The Golden Rule Revolution   Keeping in Touch by E-mail
> The Wisdom of Ponies   Eyes of the Twister
> I Remember When   The Muskrat Mysteries

1 A young girl learns lessons of life from watching the horses at her grandfather's farm.

_____

2 Two friends learn how to keep their friendship strong after one moves away.

_____

3 A photo essay presents the effects of tornadoes on midwestern towns.

_____

4 A grandmother shares her memories of childhood with her twin grandsons.

_____

5 Students learn how a small act of kindness can change everything about their school.

_____

6 Four friends spend the summer tracking down clues to solve a furry problem.

_____

Reading Skills 3–4 • © 2004 Creative Teaching Press

So Short

SUMMARIZING

A **summary** tells only the most important parts of what was read, seen, or heard. It includes only the most important main ideas.

Read each paragraph. Write a summary of it in 1–2 sentences.

Two friends decided to plan a bake sale to raise money for their local animal shelter. They each baked three dozen cookies, two dozen brownies, and five loaves of banana bread. After baking their items, they bagged them and tied each with ribbon. Two days before the event, they made three signs. The first one read, "Bake Sale: 25¢ each." The second sign read, "All money goes to the animal shelter." The third one read, "Support the Animals." On the morning of their bake sale, they put their signs up around their table at the neighborhood park. Their sale was quite a success! They raised $153.75 for the animal shelter! Every penny would help the animals. They felt so good about what they did.

Summary: _____

_____

_____

Many people in the neighborhood walked through the nature center and nearby park every day. One day, there were more people at the park than usual. Erin walked up to a man and asked him what he was looking at. The man told her that two owls had four young owlets. Since owls were so unusual in the city, Erin was excited. She took her family to see the owls. She told all of her friends about the owls. They told their friends, too. Soon, the park was filled with people trying to see live owls flying free in the city. Erin's son Maxx and his friend David loved searching for the owls and hooting for them. The owls stayed in the park trees for two months. What a treat they were for the people of the city!

Summary: _____

_____

_____

In or Out?

Summarizing

A **summary** tells only the most important parts of what was read, seen, or heard. It includes only the most important main ideas.

Read the story.

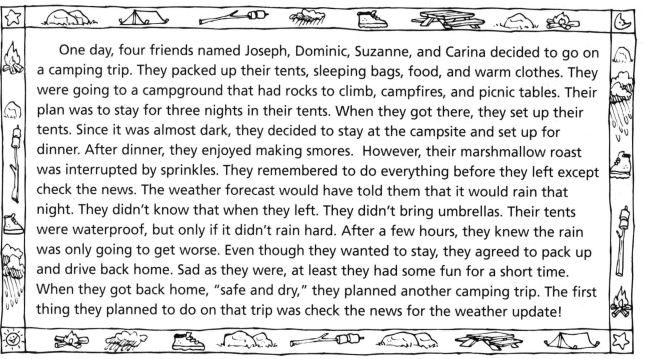

One day, four friends named Joseph, Dominic, Suzanne, and Carina decided to go on a camping trip. They packed up their tents, sleeping bags, food, and warm clothes. They were going to a campground that had rocks to climb, campfires, and picnic tables. Their plan was to stay for three nights in their tents. When they got there, they set up their tents. Since it was almost dark, they decided to stay at the campsite and set up for dinner. After dinner, they enjoyed making smores. However, their marshmallow roast was interrupted by sprinkles. They remembered to do everything before they left except check the news. The weather forecast would have told them that it would rain that night. They didn't know that when they left. They didn't bring umbrellas. Their tents were waterproof, but only if it didn't rain hard. After a few hours, they knew the rain was only going to get worse. Even though they wanted to stay, they agreed to pack up and drive back home. Sad as they were, at least they had some fun for a short time. When they got back home, "safe and dry," they planned another camping trip. The first thing they planned to do on that trip was check the news for the weather update!

Read each phrase. Write "I" on the blank next to each phrase that belongs IN a summary. Write "O" next to each phrase statements that is too detailed should be left OUT of a summary.

1 _____ Four friends went camping

2 _____ Joseph, Dominic, Suzanne, and Carina

3 _____ They packed their tents, sleeping bags, food, and warm clothes

4 _____ The campground had rocks to climb, campfires, and picnic tables

5 _____ Stay for three nights in their tents

6 _____ After dinner, they enjoyed making smores

7 _____ It rained

8 _____ They remembered to do everything except check the news

Reading Skills 3–4 • © 2004 Creative Teaching Press

Match Time

PROBLEM AND SOLUTION

A **problem** is something that makes someone think. It is usually an event that was not wanted. A **solution** is a way of solving a problem. It makes the unwanted event better in some way.

Read the list of problems in the left column. Read the list of solutions in the right column. Write the letter of the solution that best solves each problem.

Problems

1 ____ She got a spider bite.

2 ____ She woke up cold in the middle of every night.

3 ____ He sneezed every time he walked through a field or a park.

4 ____ He was allergic to peanut butter.

5 ____ Every month she was short on money and couldn't pay her bills.

6 ____ The remote control wouldn't work.

7 ____ She couldn't find her book.

8 ____ She was hungry.

9 ____ His kids wanted their own rooms.

10 ____ The words seemed blurry on the page.

Solutions

a. She borrowed one from a friend.

b. She changed the batteries.

c. She made a sandwich.

d. He bought a new house with more bedrooms.

e. He didn't eat anything made from peanuts.

f. She got glasses.

g. She wore thicker pajamas and socks to bed.

h. He took allergy medicine.

i. She put lotion on it and tried not to scratch.

j. She got a second job.

What's the Problem?

PROBLEM AND SOLUTION

Read each solution. Predict what the problem was and write it in the box.

Problems	Solutions
	She got a job.
	He went to the cupboard to find the carpet cleaner.
	She bought a new pair of tennis shoes.
	He put the ice cream back into the freezer.
	She went to the garage to get the lawn mower.
	He called the cable television company.
	She went to the nearest fast-food restaurant.
	He had the lock cut off his locker.

hmm...?

Reading Skills 3–4 • © 2004 Creative Teaching Press

What's Your Solution?

PROBLEM AND SOLUTION

Read each problem. Write a good solution to each problem.

Problems	Solutions
He got a splinter in his finger.	
She didn't read the chapter she was told to read for homework.	
His car was almost out of gas.	
Her baby was crying for almost a half hour.	
He didn't have enough money for the hamburger, fries, and shake.	
The cell phone stopped ringing before she could find it in her purse.	
The batteries in the camera were dead.	
She forgot her lunch money at home.	

I got it!

The Best Solution

Problem and Solution

Read each problem. Circle the letter of the best solution.

1 The window washer couldn't reach the top window.
a. He skipped it.
b. He got a ladder.
c. He squirted it with a hose.
d. He decided it didn't really need to be washed anyway.

2 The stapler was out of staples in the classroom.
a. The student folded the papers together.
b. The student turned in the two papers anyway.
c. The student folded the top corner of the papers.
d. The student asked the teacher for more staples.

3 The boy forgot his jacket on the playground.
a. He would wait until it showed up in the lost and found.
b. He would tell his parents that someone took it.
c. He would blame it on his friend.
d. He would look for it after school.

4 The girl lost her library book.
a. She would tell the librarian and pay for it.
b. She wouldn't go back to that library again.
c. She would say she never checked it out in the first place.
d. She would wait until she got caught.

5 The Internet connection was down.
a. She would try again later.
b. She would yell at the computer.
c. She would give up.
d. She would call the Internet company.

6 Her lemonade was getting warm and she really wanted to drink it right away.
a. She would pour it down the drain.
b. She would put it in the refrigerator.
c. She would put ice in it.
d. She would get angry.

Reading Skills 3–4 • © 2004 Creative Teaching Press

Name _____ Date _____

Whose Views?

POINT OF VIEW

The **point of view** means the opinions or thoughts of a person about a topic. How you see and think about something is different from other people.

Fill in the chart listing what your point of view would be and the point of view of one of your parents on each of the topics. Write a "+" in the last colum if your point of view would be the same. Write a "–" if it would be different.

Issue	Your point of view	Your parent's point of view	Agree?
Music to listen to			
Television shows to watch			
Clothing to wear			
Bed time			
Number of chores			
Amount of allowance			

Name _____ Date _____

Everyone Has a Different View

POINT OF VIEW

Most stories are told from the point of view of one character or a narrator. Write a short description of what you think happened from different characters' points of view. Begin each description with the word "I," since you will think like each character.

What was the real story, Little Pig? _____

_____

_____

_____

What was the real story, Wolf? _____

_____

_____

_____

What was the real story, Baby Bear? _____

_____

_____

_____

What was the real story, Goldilocks? _____

_____

_____

_____

Reading Skills 3–4 • © 2004 Creative Teaching Press

Name _____ Date _____

Who Said That?

POINT OF VIEW

If you really understand characters, then you understand their point of view, including what they would think, how they would act, and what they would do in any situation.
Read the comments in the puzzle. Identify the character from a common story based on that character's point of view. Use these names to complete the crossword puzzle.

Across

1. My stepsisters were so mean to me. They made me do all the work in the house. At least I got to live happily ever after.
2. I was shocked to find my porridge gone, my chair broken, and someone in my bed when I got home.
3. I was so good to all of the animals on the farm. I'm so lucky my good friend wrote nice things about me. She saved my life!
4. I was lucky to meet a nice girl at the ball. If she hadn't lost her shoe, who knows if we would have ever met.
5. Every story makes me out to be the bad guy. I'm innocent. I just have bad allergies. That's why I always sneeze.
8. I missed my family so much. I'm glad I got to help my friend find his courage, but it was a scary adventure!

Down

4. I didn't mean to tell lies. I tried not to. I couldn't believe it when my nose started to grow.
6. I was just skipping along with my basket full of goodies for my grandma when I thought I heard someone following me. The next day, I was shocked!
7. I worked so hard to save my friend's life. Writing in webs is no easy task!
9. I was just trying to find out who lived in the beautiful house. I was lonely. I shouldn't have eaten their breakfast. I should have knocked on their door first.

Reading Skills 3–4 • © 2004 Creative Teaching Press

Name _____ Date _____

Put Yourself in Other People's Shoes

POINT OF VIEW

The saying "Put yourself in my shoes" means for you to think about a situation from another person's point of view. Describe the first day back at school from the point of view of four different people.

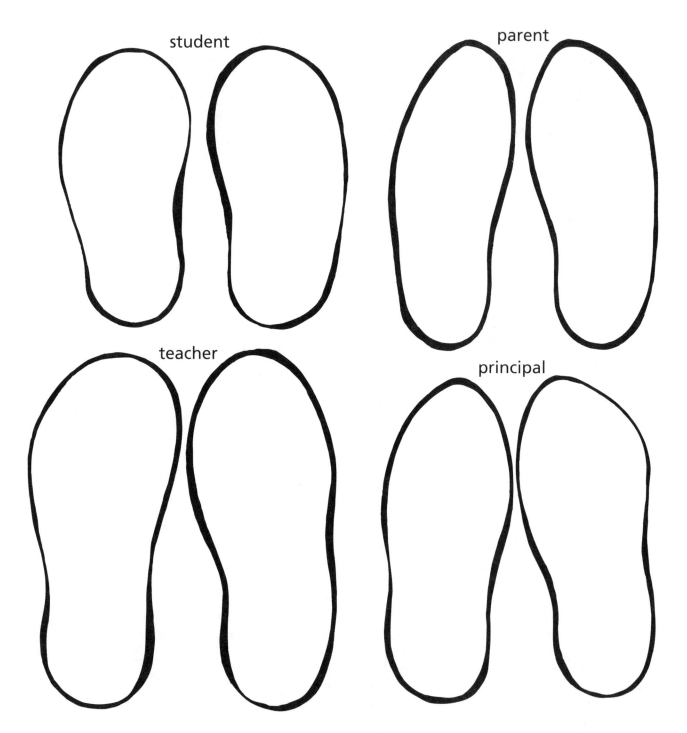

student

parent

teacher

principal

First or Third Person?

Point of View

Books are written in the first or third person point of view.
First person point of view is when the narrator of the story is a main character.
    Example: "I couldn't sleep last night. I kept thinking about Stuart."
Third person point of view is when the narrator is an outsider. The story is not told by a character.
    Example: "Malcolm couldn't sleep that night. He kept thinking about Stuart."

Read each sentence. Identify whether it would most likely be told in first or third person point of view in a story.

First   Third   **1**   Timothy was very ill. His mother went to Mr. Ages to ask for some medicine.

First   Third   **2**   At that moment, Kendra and Garrett began riding their bikes.

First   Third   **3**   Five seconds ago, I would have guessed it was my mother knocking on my bedroom door.

First   Third   **4**   Arthur was so busy building the brick wall that he didn't even hear the phone ring.

First   Third   **5**   Shocked, I walked back through the secret passage.

First   Third   **6**   Many people didn't believe me when the story finally came out.

First   Third   **7**   My best friend found the missing letters.

First   Third   **8**   They were surprised to find the golden coin.

First   Third   **9**   Before my eyes, I saw the most amazing view of the garden! It reminded me of my homeland.

First   Third   **10**   Where else could I go? I had no choice! I was stuck!

What did you notice? _____

_____

_____

Name _____ Date _____

Cool Careers

COMPARE AND CONTRAST

To **compare** is to find things that are the same. To **contrast** is to find things that are different.

Compare and contrast the jobs with the descriptions. If a career matches a description, put a star in the box. If a career and a description do not match, put a "–" in the box.

Description	Police Officer	Teacher	Tow Truck Driver	Veterinarian	Chef
must graduate from college					
helps people					
helps animals					
dangerous job					
saves lives					
needs special training					
needs special equipment					
is something you'd enjoy					

Reading Skills 3–4 • © 2004 Creative Teaching Press

Name _____ Date _____

Images

COMPARE AND CONTRAST

Look at the two pictures carefully. There are at least ten similarities and ten differences. List as many as you can find in the Venn diagram.

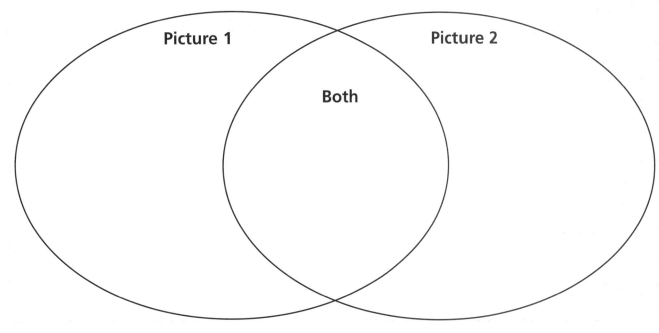

Picture 1	Picture 2

Picture 1   Picture 2

Both

Common Things

Compare and Contrast

Look at each pair of items. Write at least three ways that they are similar and three ways they are different.

Similarities		Differences

Layers of Earth

Compare and Contrast

Read the paragraph about the earth's mantle and core. Fill in the Venn diagram with as many similarities and differences as you can find in the paragraph.

There are three layers to the earth: the crust, mantle, and core. The crust is the outer rock layer on which we live. It is rich in oxygen and silicon. The middle layer is the mantle. It is located between the crust and the core. The mantle is a layer of rock. It is made up of minerals rich in iron, silicon, magnesium, and oxygen. There are three sections of the mantle. The temperatures in the mantle are hotter than the crust. The inner layer of the earth is called the core. The temperatures are even hotter here. There are two sections to the core: the inner core and outer core. The outer core is made up of melted iron and nickel. The inner core is made up of solid iron and nickel. When a volcano erupts, it is the hot molten rock that bubbles to the surface from the inner core. The pressure builds up and sends the molten lava through the mantle and out the earth's crust.

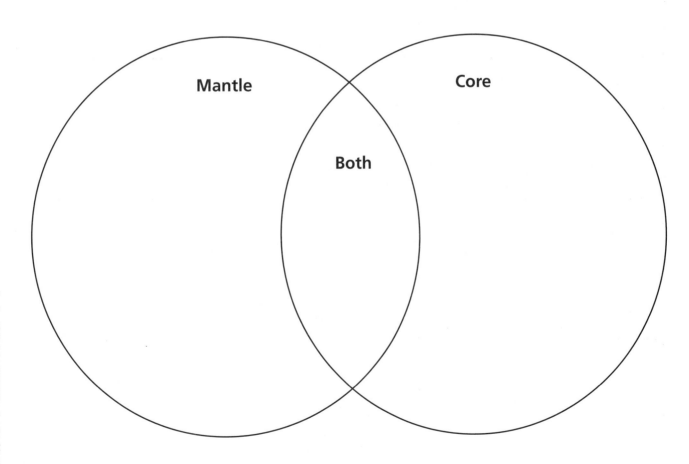

Name _____ Date _____

Many Connections

MAKING CONNECTIONS

> You are making connections when you compare how something in your book is similar to something else. There are three types of connections.
> **book-to-book**—you compare something about your book to another book
> **book-to-self**—you compare something in your book to your own life
> **book-to-world**—you compare something in your book to something on television, in a magazine, a game, or something else in the world outside of your own life

Read each comment a child made after reading a book. Identify whether it was a book-to-book, book-to-self, or book-to-world connection.

1 The main character in the story reminds me of my little brother because he is always getting food all over his face when he eats.
      a. book-to-book   **b.** book-to-self   **c.** book-to-world

2 The book reminded me of The Three Little Pigs because the pigs had to keep outsmarting the wolf just like the boy had to keep outsmarting his friend in my book.
      a. book-to-book   **b.** book-to-self   **c.** book-to-world

3 The park in the story reminds me of the park by my house. There's a duck pond at my park just like the one in the story.
      a. book-to-book   **b.** book-to-self   **c.** book-to-world

4 I think I have a video game that takes place in medieval times just like the story.
      a. book-to-book   **b.** book-to-self   **c.** book-to-world

5 My book reminds me of a television show I saw about horses. The horse on TV was in races just like in my book.
      a. book-to-book   **b.** book-to-self   **c.** book-to-world

6 I tried making a homework machine once just like the boy in my book. Mine didn't work either.
      a. book-to-book   **b.** book-to-self   **c.** book-to-world

7 The car in the book reminds me of one I saw at the Auto Expo last month. They were both red, fast, and had flip up doors.
      a. book-to-book   **b.** book-to-self   **c.** book-to-world

Character Chains

MAKING CONNECTIONS

A **character connection** is when you compare characters from two different books.

Everyone knows the stories of Little Red Riding Hood and The Three Bears. Little Red Riding Hood and Goldilocks are similar in many ways. List five ways that the two main characters are the same. How are they connected? Write each idea on the chain connecting the two characters.

Similar Settings

MAKING CONNECTIONS

A **setting connection** is when you compare where a scene, event, or whole story takes place in one book with another book.

The settings of the *Wizard of Oz* and *Charlie and the Chocolate Factory* were full of fantastic characters, images, details, and unusual objects. Draw a picture of what you pictured in each story (or movie if you've seen it).

The Wizard of Oz

Charlie and the Chocolate Factory

List four things the settings of both books have in common.

1 _____

2 _____

3 _____

4 _____

Name _____ Date _____

Book-to-Self Connections

MAKING CONNECTIONS

> A **book-to-self** connection is when you compare something in your book to your own life.

Compare the book you are reading right now to your own life. Fill in the chart.

The Character _____	r e m i n d s	_____	b e c a u s e	_____
The setting in the _____				
The part when _____ _____ _____	m e o f	_____		_____

Name _____ Date _____

Book-to-World Connections

MAKING CONNECTIONS

A **book-to-world** connection is when you compare something in your book to something on television, a magazine, a game, or something else in the world outside of your own life.

Make four book-to-world connections between the book you are reading right now and the outside world. List one connection in each shape of the world.

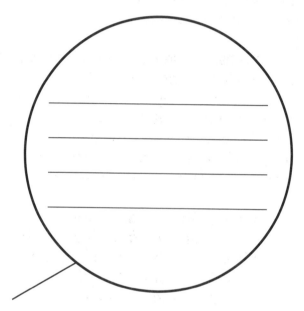

Book-to-World
Connections

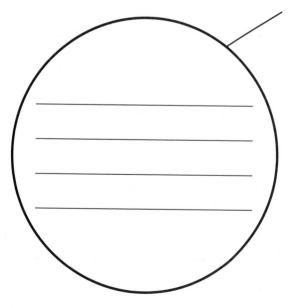

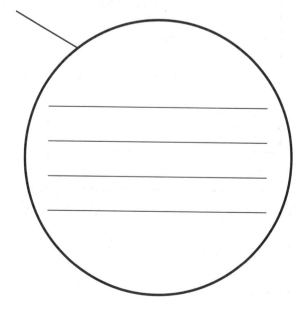

Reading Skills 3–4 • © 2004 Creative Teaching Press

Deduction Puzzle: Working Pigs

INFERENCES

An **inference** is when you use logical thinking to evaluate information and make a judgment. Clues help you to assume different things about the story.

Read the story and then the clues. As you read the clues, try to match each pig with a job. When you find a match, color that box green. The rest of the boxes in that row and column can be colored red, since each pig has only one job. If you identify a job that doesn't match a pig, then color that box red as well.

Colby, Shanelle, Combo, and Shasty are the four little pigs in a funny twist of a tale similar to The Three Little Pigs. Their mother has sent them off to build homes of their own. They know the story about their cousins and what happened to them. They've heard that the wolf is coming to their town next. They must each build a "wolf proof" home. However, the materials they need are expensive. Therefore, they each took a job to earn money. The jobs they chose were based on what they were good at while at home with Mother Pig.

Clue 1: Shasty had a sweet tooth, so he decided to take a job where he could enjoy a free snack on his breaks.

Clue 2: Combo was not good at organizing things, alphabetical order, or building things.

Clue 3: Shanelle was always in charge of putting the bills in the right monthly sections when she lived at home. She also didn't like getting her hooves dirty.

	Waiter/ Waitress	Construction Worker	File Clerk	Ice Cream Store Clerk
Colby				
Shanelle				
Combo				
Shasty				

What do you infer that each pig in the family did to earn money for his or her home?

Colby was a _____.   Combo was a _____.

Shanelle was a _____.   Shasty was a _____.

Name _____ Date _____

Deduction Puzzle: Forgetful Friends

INFERENCES

An **inference** is when you use logical thinking to evaluate information and make a judgment. Clues help you to assume different things about the story.

Read the story and then the clues. As you read the clues, try to match each friend with an item. When you find a match, color that box green. The rest of the boxes in that row and column can be colored red, since each friend forgot only one item. If you identify an item that doesn't match a friend, then color that box red as well.

On the same day, four friends forgot an item they were supposed to bring to school. They were famous for forgetting things. That's how they got the nickname "The Forgetful Friends." Their real names were Fred, Frannie, Froid, and Frita. Read the clues to figure out what each friend forgot.

Clue 1: Fred had trouble during reading and writing time, but he was all set when it was math.

Clue 2: Frannie was worried that her grade might go down.

Clue 3: Froid remembered his ruler and his homework.

Clue 4: Frita's teacher had to loan her an item during reading time.

Clue 5: Froid couldn't believe he forgot the item he uses every single day in school.

	Pencil	Ruler	Book	Homework
Fred				
Frannie				
Froid				
Frita				

What do you infer that each friend forgot?

Fred forgot a _____.

Frannie forgot a _____.

Froid forgot a _____.

Frita forgot a _____.

Reading Skills 3–4 • © 2004 Creative Teaching Press

Name _____ Date _____

Inference Ice Cream

INFERENCES

Read each set of clues. Based on the clues and your background knowledge, infer what the object is. Write its name on the ice-cream cone.

1
It has seeds.
It is eaten.
It is heavy.

2
It clicks.
It is moved by hand.
It is part of a computer.

3
It lives in a pond.
It flies.
It lays eggs.

4
It carries clothes.
It can zip.
It can be locked.

5
It is a planet.
It is red.
It is fourth.

6
It is cold.
It is white.
It freezes.

7
It is a liquid.
It is healthy.
It is clear.

Name _____ Date _____

Movie Mania

INFERENCES

Read each movie title. Decide what type of movie it probably is. Explain why.

1 *Ten Ways to Make You Smile*
type of movie: action   adventure   cartoon   comedy   scary movie
Why? _____
_____

2 *Touchdown!*
type of movie: action   adventure   cartoon   comedy   scary movie
Why? _____
_____

3 *Voyage to Venus*
type of movie: action   adventure   cartoon   comedy   scary movie
Why? _____
_____

4 *Finding the Tomb*
type of movie: action   adventure   cartoon   comedy   scary movie
Why? _____
_____

5 *The Last Ghost*
type of movie: action   adventure   cartoon   comedy   scary movie
Why? _____
_____

6 *Rodeo Roundup*
type of movie: action   adventure   cartoon   comedy   scary movie
Why? _____
_____

7 *Walking in Wackyville*
type of movie: action   adventure   cartoon   comedy   scary movie
Why? _____
_____

8 *Bugs Goes to Hollywood*
type of movie: action   adventure   cartoon   comedy   scary movie
Why? _____
_____

Reading Skills 3–4 • © 2004 Creative Teaching Press

Name _____ Date _____

Mystery of the Missing Peanuts

INFERENCES

Read the mystery. Solve the Mystery of the Missing Peanuts by answering the questions and using your ability to make inferences. You will not find the answers directly in the story. You must use what you know combined with the clues to solve this mystery.

"So the bag of peanuts is missing?" asked Detective Finder.

"It certainly is. I just don't know what I'm going to do. My class can't do the experiment without those peanuts," said Ms. Baffled.

"Please tell me the last time you saw them," replied Detective Finder patiently.

"Well, I brought them with me this morning in my bag. I set down my bag outside my door while I looked for my keys. I forgot that the bag was outside until recess. That's when I went to put the peanuts on the trays for the experiment, but I couldn't find the bag. I got the bag and brought it inside. When I opened my bag, the peanuts were missing."

"How many peanuts did you have?" asked the detective.

"I had exactly 15 in a paper sack. That way each pair of students could have one for the experiment," Ms. Baffled answered.

"Let's take a look outside. Perhaps we'll find a clue."

Ms. Baffled said, "Look! There are peanut shells all over the ground, but no peanuts! There seems to be a trail of shells leading over to those trees right there."

Detective Finder said, 'You're right. It's a good thing it's a beautiful fall day so we can see the trail easily in all this grass. You sure have a beautiful view here."

"Yes, we do. We're very lucky to have such a fine country school. Where do you think the trail leads and where are my peanuts?" asked Ms. Baffled

Detective Finder replied, "I think we're about to find out!"

1 Where exactly did the story take place? How do you know? _____

_____

2 What was the problem? _____

_____

3 What time of day was it? How do you know? _____

_____

4 Where do you think the peanuts went? Explain completely. _____

_____

5 What clues helped you solve the mystery? _____

_____

Reading Skills 3–4 • © 2004 Creative Teaching Press

Name _____ Date _____

Interesting Inferences

INFERENCES

Read each scenario. Write what was probably happening in each scene using your knowledge and the clues.

1 Many people were gathered around the girl. A red truck just pulled up. People ran out of the red truck. The girl was crying. Someone was picking up the pieces of her bike. What happened? _____

_____

2 The class was eating cupcakes. They were singing a song. Someone was blushing. What was happening? _____

_____

3 There was screaming. There was laughing. Some people even had their eyes start to water. Hair was flying everywhere. People were holding onto bars across their laps. What was happening? _____

_____

4 People were dressed in thick jackets and boots. People were scraping the windows of their cars. Most people tried to stay inside. What was happening? _____

_____

5 People were asking for candy. People were wandering up and down the streets everywhere in the city. It was dark. People were knocking on doors. What was happening? _____

_____

6 Two people were running back and forth. They were swinging something in their arms. A ball was bouncing back and forth. What was happening?

_____

_____

Reading Skills 3–4 • © 2004 Creative Teaching Press

Word Choice

Confusing Words

Circle the word that correctly completes each sentence.

1 (Its, It's) going to be a beautiful day.

2 Lisa (passed, past) her plate to her mom.

3 Sacramento is the (capital, capitol) of California.

4 (Their, There) are many students in my class.

5 It was her turn to (role, roll) the dice.

6 Maria is shorter (than, then) Michael.

7 I (already, all ready) turned in my homework.

8 I wonder what the (weather, whether) will be like today.

9 Mrs. Maki is the (principal, principle) of our school.

10 She sold (fewer, less) cookies than her friend.

11 Our team practiced so we would not (loose, lose) the game.

12 The bride walked down the (isle, aisle).

Make the Right Choice

CONFUSING WORDS

Read each situation. Then draw an X in front of the correct choice.

1 Michelle has been babysitting for her neighbor all summer. She would like to earn more money during the school year. She wants to know if her neighbor could pay her more money each week. What should she do?

_____ She should ask for a rise.

_____ She should ask for a raise.

2 Jamal has a habit of dropping his coat and books at the door when he comes home from school. His mother would like him to be more responsible with his things. What should his mother say to him?

____ Please lay your things in your room.

____ Please lie your things in your room.

3 The cafeteria posts the lunch menu on a board in the school office. Which of the following items is correct?

_____ Desert will be an apple and a cookie.

_____ Dessert will be an apple and a cookie.

4 The library posted a notice to remind students that talking was not permitted. What should be written on this notice?

_____ Please remember to be quite in the library.

_____ Please remember to be quiet in the library.

Name _____ Date _____

Which Is Correct

CONFUSING WORDS

Read each sentence. Circle **C** if the underlined word is used correctly or **I** if it is used incorrectly.

1 C   I   The medicine will have an immediate <u>affect</u> on her headache.

2 C   I   Scrapbooks are a nice way to remember the <u>past</u>.

3 C   I   The teachers and principal are part of the school <u>personnel</u>.

4 C   I   The lid on the mild container was <u>loose</u>.

5 C   I   We took a field trip to the <u>capital</u> building.

6 C   I   I will need to pay back the <u>loan</u> in thirty days.

7 C   I   <u>Accept</u> for my brother, my whole family wears glasses.

8 C   I   You must turn on the machine, and <u>then</u> push the button.

9 C   I   She was <u>conscious</u> of the noise in the background.

10 C   I   The sun <u>raises</u> each morning at 6:00 a.m.

11 C   I   I found the money <u>laying</u> in the street.

12 C   I   I read the <u>biography</u> of Abraham Lincoln.

13 C   I   The criminal <u>devised</u> a plan for escape.

14 C   I   How <u>good</u> do you know my uncle?

Definition Match

CONFUSING WORDS

Match each word with the correct definition.

1 ____ except   **a.** to change or adjust

2 ____ accept   **b.** a small island

3 ____ stationery   **c.** a rule or code of conduct

4 ____ stationary   **d.** occurring twice a year

5 ____ adapt   **e.** immovable

6 ____ adopt   **f.** a passageway between sections of seats

7 ____ aisle   **g.** to receive as one's own

8 ____ isle   **h.** to receive

9 ____ annual   **i.** a chief or head man or woman

10 ____ biannual   **j.** paper for writing a letter

11 ____ principal   **k.** occurring yearly

12 ____ principle   **l.** not including

Reading Skills 3–4 • © 2004 Creative Teaching Press

Answer Key

Add 'Em Up! (page 5)

1. barnyard
2. backbone
3. courtroom
4. football
5. homework
6. pinecone
7. underwear
8. scarecrow
9. waterproof
10. suitcase
11. backstroke or breaststroke
12. greenhouse

Compound Crossword (page 6)

Across
1. backpack 2. sailboat 4. lifeguard
5. skyscraper 7. indoor 9. fingernail 11. teapot
Down
3. earthquake 6. doorknob 8. newspaper 12. playground

Compound Word Search (page 7)

Students should circle and list 8 of these words.
underwear, storybook, bedroom, vineyard, bookmark, daydream, snowstorm, hallway, haircut, airplane, flagpole, halftime

Compound Collections (page 8)

Answers will vary. Possible answers include:

endless	timeless	groundless
useless	headlight	anytime
anymore	anyplace	overhead
moreover	overuse	headless
understood	undergo	sometime
underground	overtime	someplace
overhear		

Simple Similes (page 9)

1. He was <u>as funny as a comedian</u>.
2. She was <u>as hungry as a horse</u>.
3. They were <u>as wild as a pair of monkeys</u>.
4. He acted <u>like a frightened rabbit</u>.
5. Isn't that painting <u>as colorful as a rainbow</u>?
6. The players are <u>as fast as an airplane</u>.
7. His letter was <u>as priceless as a treasure</u>.
8. She was <u>as smart as a teacher</u>.

9. The experiment was <u>as explosive as a volcano</u>.
10. She was <u>like an elephant</u> the way she ate so many peanuts.
11. The baby was <u>as cute as a button</u>.
12. Joey thought the job was <u>as easy as pie</u>.
13. Kim felt <u>as sick as a dog</u> after she ate ten hot dogs.
14. Playing chess with my dad <u>is like trying to outsmart a computer</u>.
15. Billy was <u>as stubborn as a mule</u>.

Simile Match-Up (page 10)

1. g
2. l
3. b
4. i
5. o
6. c
7. e
8. j
9. f
10. a
11. h
12. d
13. m
14. n
15. k

Metaphors (page 11)

1. Your <u>education</u> is the <u>gateway to success</u>.
2. <u>Her life</u> is a <u>rollercoaster</u> of events.
3. <u>Dad's beard</u> was a <u>prickly porcupine</u>.
4. His mother thought <u>he</u> was being a <u>pain in the neck</u>.
5. She said, "<u>My brother</u> is such <u>a clown</u>."
6. <u>Chris</u> was a <u>walking encyclopedia</u>.
7. The shy <u>girl</u> became a <u>graceful swan</u> when she danced.
8. We would have had more to eat if <u>Tyler</u> hadn't been such a <u>hog</u>.

Simile or Metaphor (page 12)

1. S
2. M
3. S
4. M
5. S
6. M
7. S
8. M

9. M
10. S
11. M
12. M
13. S
14. S
15. S

Hooray for Homophones (page 13)

1. whole
2. they're, their
3. which
4. here
5. night
6. knot
7. close
8. days
9. dear
10. side
11. tied
12. week/whole
13. would
14. read/days
15. pour
16. pause
17. won
18. lead

Homophone Crossword Fun (page 14)

Across

1. scent
2. cent
3. ferry
4. fairy
5. hire
6. higher
7. dew
8. due

Down

3. flew
4. flu
6. hole
9. whole
10. towed
11. toad

What Does It Mean? (page 15)

1. j
2. p
3. f
4. m
5. g
6. o
7. b
8. l
9. n
10. e
11. d
12. h
13. k
14. c
15. a
16. i

Unscramble It (page 16)

1. wind
2. whined
3. toad
4. towed
5. tales
6. tails
7. scene
8. seen
9. rays
10. raise

Paired Up (page 17)

Answers will vary. Possible answers include:
funny—humorous, comical
happy—joyful, glad, content
stop—cease, halt, finish
hard—firm, solid, stiff
calm—serene, still, peaceful
brave—courageous, bold, valiant
announce—reveal, proclaim, state
create—make, produce, build
terrific—fantastic, great
cost—price, rate, fee
easy—simple, effortless
dangerous—unsafe, risky

Super Sentences (page 18)

Answers will vary. Possible answers include:
1. yummy, delicious, tasty

2. assistance, a hand
3. difficult, challenging
4. excited, thrilled
5. chilly, nippy
6. kind, friendly
7. lovely, beautiful
8. enjoy, have fun
9. speedy, swift
10. large, bulky
11. terrific, an outstanding
12. an enjoyable, pleasant
13. foolish, ridiculous
14. present, reward
15. complete, conclude

Antonym Crossword (page 19)

Across

1. answer
2. straight
3. above
4. stop
6. tall
8. lose
10. laugh
11. near

Down

1. adult
3. after
4. sister
5. noisy
7. south
8. left
9. true
10. last

Antonym Match-Up (page 20)

1. h
2. c
3. l
4. e
5. n
6. a
7. f
8. i
9. o
10. k
11. m
12. b
13. g

14. d
15. j

Find the Synonyms and Antonyms (page 21)

1. untrue
2. well
3. assist
4. simple
5. inexpensive
6. dirty
7. incorrect
8. warn
9. want
10. renew
11. admit
12. break
13. temporary
14. many
15. walk
16. start
17. difference
18. mean

Solve the Riddle (page 22)

You plug its nose with a clothespin.

Hidden Truck (page 23)

e	i	o	dd	u	i	ef	a	fp	u
a	u	e	i	b	d	f	h	p	r
lh	zs	tw	tr	m	k	j	s	g	l
e	o	gr	cr	n	g	d	p	h	r
mn	a	cl	br	v	t	q	k	n	s
◆	ch	sw	dr	d	j	f	s	g	c
u	st	19	bl	m	w	z	b	4	f
kk	6	42	2	vw	zx	bg	8	5	9
rr	ih	3	i	wq	a	op	u	11	hj
kd	e	ns	ou	o	fd	u	tz	i	pp

Sports (page 24)

Column A	Column B
	Answers will vary. Possible answers include:
baseball	bat, mitt, baseball
basketball	hoop, court
football	goal post, football
golf	tee, golf clubs
gymnastics	uneven bars, balance beam
hockey	puck, ice
soccer	goal, field

surfing	waves, surfboard
tennis	tennis racquet, tennis ball
volleyball	net, kneepads

What's My Name? (page 25)

Ferdinand Magellan

What Tools Do We Need? (page 26)

Answers may vary. Possible answers include:
1. saw, hammer
2. judge
3. weaver
4. books
5. scientist
6. whistle
7. oven
8. hoe, hose, shovel
9. doctor
10. hair stylist, barber
11. author, writer
12. ship captain
13. housekeeper, parent
14. speaker, presenter
Individual analogies will vary.

Synonym and Antonym Analogies (page 27)

Answers may vary. Possible answers include:
1. happy
2. carry
3. annoy, badger, bother
4. full
5. early
6. record
7. solution
8. find
9. cheap, inexpensive
10. car
11. try
12. loud
13. angry
14. wet

Grammar Analogies (page 28)

1. happy
2. pre
3. ate
4. which
5. slept
6. yours
7. children
8. oxen
9. seller
10. smartest
11. mice
12. brighter
13. sub
14. she
15. pause
Individual analogies will vary.

Mixed Analogies Word Search (page 29)

1. left
2. night
3. metal
4. soup
5. head
6. flies
7. people
8. red
9. plane
10. county
11. bear
12. sty

Get in Shape with Analogies (page 30)

1. vegetable
2. liquid
3. chin
4. blades
5. closet
6. cold
7. week
8. school
9. flower
10. here

What's in a Name? (page 31)

Answers may vary. Possible answers include:
Expeditious Internet because it is the fastest Internet connection and "expeditious" means acting promptly and efficiently.
Humorous High Jinks because the movie is a comedy so it is probably humorous.
Multicolor 4000 since the machine can print many different colors.
Serenity since the dog is calm and friendly. "Serenity"

means calm and "spry" means lively or active.
Tranquility since you want a restful stay. "Tranquility"
means calm and "uproarious" means noisy.
Wise Ones because the game is supposed to make kids
smarter.

Dictionary Damage (page 32)

1. children
2. device
3. addition
4. bones
5. liquid
6. money
7. topic
8. life
9. division
10. main
11. take
12. machine

Words in Words (page 33)

Answers will vary. Possible answers include:
3-Letter Words—ace, and, ant, ate, cat, cod, cot, cue, cut,
die, dot, doe, due, duo, eat, end, ion, nod, nut, oat, ode,
one, out, tea, ten, tie, tin, ton, toe
4-Letter Words—aced, acne, aide, anti, aunt, auto, cane,
cite, coat, code, coin, date, dent, diet, dice, done, duct,
dune, icon, iced, idea, into, neat, nice, once, taco, tide, tied,
toad, toed, tone, tune, undo, unit, unto
5-Letter Words—acted, acute, atone, canoe, count, edict,
noted, ocean, ounce, tonic, toned, tunic, untie
More Than 5 Letters—auction, caution, cautioned, coated,
coined, deacon, decant, detain, docent, donate, induct,
notice, noticed, octane, toucan, united
Secret Word—EDUCATION

Newsworthy Vocabulary (page 34)

Anwers may vary slighty.
News—president, agreement, elections, treaty
Sports—soccer, touchdown, finals
Weather—cloudy, thunderstorms, barometer, radar
Entertainment—comics, theater, plays, movies, television
Money—budget, banks, companies, stocks

Reading Materials Match-Up (page 35)

1. f
2. b
3. i
4. d
5. a
6. g
7. j
8. e
9. c
10. h

Comprehension (page 36)

1. vocabulary
2. strategies
3. sequence
4. retell
5. inference
6. opinion
7. compare
8. contrast

Why? (page 37)

Answers will vary.

How? (page 38)

Answers will vary.

Your Book or Your Head? (page 39)

1. book
2. head
3. book
4. head
5. head
6. book
7. book
8. head
9. book
10. head
11. head
12. book

Some or All? (page 40)

1. False
2. True
3. True
4. False
5. False
6. False

7. False
8. True
9. True
10. False
11. False
12. False
13. True
14. True
15. True

Indoor Smores (page 41)

1. mini marshmallows, corn syrup, chocolate chips
2. they melt
3. 16
4. 6 cups
5. so the smores don't stick to the dish
6. let them cool completely

Sturdy Windsock (page 42)

1. let the glue dry
2. craft foam, hot glue gun or wood glue, hole punch, raffia, yarn, staples
3. to blow in the wind
4. blow in the breeze
5. they are stronger and hold better than school glue
6. foam is more sturdy than paper while blowing in the wind

Multiplication Race (page 43)

1. practice multiplication
2. two
3. multiply numerals on dice
4. the person who rolls an even number
5. divide, add, positive/negative numbers, subtract

Mint Ice Cream (page 44)

1. friction helps freeze the ingredients; ice rolls around the ingredients freezing them
2. peppermint and peppermint sticks
3. ice and rock salt
4. so they don't change the flavor of the ice cream
5. empty the cans and do it again; get 4 cans

Follow That Recipe (page 45)

1. 2
2. milk, sugar, vanilla
3. 5 minutes
4. 6. Put the bag in the freezer.
   2. Put ice in a large freezer bag.
   4. Put the small bag in large bag.
   1. Put milk, sugar, and vanilla in small plastic bag.
   3. Add salt to the ice.
   5. Shake the bag.
5. 3/4 tablespoon

Sort It Out (page 46)

Things you wear—sock, hat, muff, ring
Colors—tan, red, turquoise, magenta
Parts of the body—leg, lung, rib, neck
Weather words—wind, chill, fog, mist

Book Categories (page 47)

1. Famous People
2. Humor
3. Mystery
4. Instructional Guide
5. Sports
6. Humor
7. Mystery
8. Science
9. Sports
10. Instructional Guide
11. Famous People
12. Science

Sort the Words (page 48)

States—Florida, Texas, Ohio, New York
Continents—Asia, Africa, Europe, Australia
Things to Wear—helmet, sneakers, coat, jersey
Things to Read—magazine, letter, brochure, essay, diary
Weather—thunder, fog, hail, sleet
Habitats—tundra, ocean, desert, prairie

Odd One Out (page 49)

1. Georgian—not a Native American tribe
2. number—not a shape
3. classroom—not a subject
4. sheet—not a piece of clothing
5. country—not a body of water
6. moon—not on Earth
7. lasagna—not a dessert
8. sofa—not something you cook in
9. man—not an adjective

10. late—not a synonym for "ready"
11. legend—not a cardinal direction
12. friendly—not a word describing a rushed crowd
13. fish—not eaten by herbivores OR hay–not eaten by humans
14. penny—not silver in color
15. America—not a continent

Balanced Thinking (page 50)

Answers will vary. Possible answers include:
1. carrots (or another vegetable)
2. apple (or another fruit)
3. cheetah (something that is very fast)
4. peanuts (baseball game food)
5. fastener (something that seals)
6. boots (something worn or put on the feet)
7. cap (something worn or put on the head)
8. antiques (something that is collected)

TV Time (page 51)

1. The History Station
2. Animal Network
3. Cartoon Channel
4. Fashion Fun
5. The Classics
6. Game Shows
7. Cooking Channel
8. Technology Today

Main Idea Tree Diagram (page 52)

Answers may vary. Possible answers include:
1. Goldilocks didn't follow the safety rules.
2. Happy people make other people happy.
3. Some people don't like change.

What's the Topic? (page 53)

1. Pluto
2. Country Music
3. Pollution
4. Sir Isaac Newton

Headlines (page 54)

1. The Destructive Storm
2. Pets Help People
3. Beating the Odds

The Main Idea (page 55)

Answers will vary. Possible answers include:
1. Rainbows are beautiful visions.
2. I saw so many wonderful things on my trip to the rain forest.
3. I had an eventful day at the zoo.
4. I have many chores to do each week.
5. My favorite food is pizza.
6. My best friend Tonya and I do many things together.

Comic Capers (page 56)

Answers will vary. Possible answers include:
1. The family builds a fire and cooks dinner.
2. The man drives off in his new car.
3. The girl's parents help her clean up the mess.

Picture Prediction (page 57)

1. Zoo Clues
2. Baseball Greats
3. Delicious Dinner Dishes
4. Technology Tricks
5. The Berry Bunch
6. The Case of the Missing Teacher

Predict a Book (page 58)

Answers will vary.

What Is That Web Site? (page 59)

Answers will vary. Possible answers include:
1. draw or paint
2. buy a sofa
3. play logic games
4. make money, save money, get money tips
5. watch cartoons, read cartoons, download cartoons
6. get homework help
7. sign up for books, magazines, etc.
8. find a job
9. buy video games

What Will Happen? (page 60)

Answers will vary. Possible answers include:
1. The teacher will make the student complete his homework during recess.
2. Mr. Rish decides to take the bus to work.
3. Ms. Smith was late for work.
4. The cat's owner wakes up to help the cat.

5. The head of the company is fired.

6. Many people go to the store to buy sale items.

7. The price of the Talking Toto toy goes up and it is hard to find.

8. More people purchase DVD players.

5. hero
6. problems
7. beginning
8. middle
9. main ideas
11. details
10. end
12. villain

Good or Evil? (page 61)

1. down
2. down
3. up
4. down
5. down
6. up
7. up
8. down
9. down
10. down
11. down
12. up
13. up
14. up
15. up

What a Character! (page 62)

1. Charlie
2. Baby Bear
3. Hare
4. Wolf
5. Cinderella
6. Pinocchio
7. Giant
8. Humpty Dumpty

Get Set (page 63)

playground or sandbox

mountains or ski resort

rain forest

volcano or national park

Which Setting? (page 64)

Answers will vary.

Parts of a Story Crossword (page 65)

Across	Down
1. characters	2. setting
4. plot	3. solutions

The Basic Idea (page 66)

a. 2, 1, 3, 4
b. 1, 4, 2, 3 (may vary)
c. 3, 1, 2, 4 (may vary)
d. 1, 2, 4, 3
e. 2, 1, 3, 4
f. 4, 1, 3, 2
g. 2, 4, 1, 3
h. 1, 2, 4, 3

Order It (page 67)

Laundry Day—5, 4, 2, 3, 1

Sending a Letter—2, 5, 3, 1, 4

Making Hot Chocolate—5, 3, 1, 4, 2

Going to Bed—3, 5, 1, 2, 4

In What Order? (page 68)

(Answers may vary)

The Picnic in the Park—3, 4, 1, 2, 6, 5

The Television Studio—5, 2, 4, 6, 1, 3, 7

Grandma's Cookies—3, 4, 1, 2, 5

The Sleepover—7, 2, 4, 6, 3, 1, 5

Story Ordering (page 69)

1. 3, 5, 1, 4, 2
2. 4, 2, 5, 3, 1
3. 3, 1, 5, 2, 4

Note Card Nightmare (page 70)

1—I was born early in the morning on Thanksgiving Day.

2—My favorite animal when I was a baby was a teddy bear that sang when you squeezed it.

3—My brother was born when I was 5.

4—I began taking piano lessons at age 7.

5—My dad coached…

6—The summer after winning…

7—I got braces and glasses in 6th grade.

8—My favorite teacher was…

New Words (page 71)

1. compass
2. move
3. arguing
4. noise
5. angry
6. nibble

Finish the Story (page 72)

1. believing
2. assisting
3. ordinary
4. discovered
5. neglected
6. definitely
7. shiny
8. ancient
9. genuine
10. amazement
11. vibrating
12. ridiculous

Figure It Out (page 73)

Answers will vary. Possible answers include:

enormous—large, huge
terrified—to be scared
destruction—great damage
ravenous—greedy for food
heroine—brave woman or girl
disintegrate—break up into many pieces
vanish—disappear
eliminated—removed or gotten rid of

Context Clues Crossword (page 74)

Across

1. relax
3. fearless
4. decide
5. alone
7. complicated

Down

2. awkward
3. foolish
4. dispute
6. wanted
7. control
8. bad

What Else Fits? (page 75)

1. c
2. a
3. b
4. d
5. d
6. a
7. b
8. c

Many Effects (page 76)

Answers will vary.

Many Possible Causes (page 77)

Answers will vary.

Causes and Effects (page 78)

1. The (children froze) on the playground when they heard the bell ring.
2. Since the bill was late (she had to pay a fine.)
3. (They went down the waterslide) to cool off on the hot summer day.
4. (They threw the balloon away) after it popped
5. Before going on a walk, she (put the leash on her dog.)
6. (She had a stomachache) after eating too many pieces of candy.
7. He fell off his bike and (cut his knee.)
8. (The television went off) when electricity went out.
9. (The car stopped) when it reached the red light.
10. When the movie let out, the (people left the theater.)
11. (Glass was all over the floor) after she dropped the picture frame.
12. He was pleased to see that (he had lost five pounds) by running on the treadmill daily for a week.
13. (She was twitching in her sleep) since she was dreaming.
14. (He sneezed) because he had bad allergies.
15. (She bought a new toothbrush) because hers was getting old.

Match 'Em Up (page 79)

1. j
2. e
3. h
4. a
5. b
6. d
7. g
8. c
9. f
10. i

Sentences will vary.

If...Then (page 80)

1. a
2. b
3. d
4. c
5. c
6. d

Fact or Opinion? (page 81)

1. O
2. O
3. F
4. F
5. O
6. F
7. O
8. O
9. F
10. F
11. O
12. F
13. O
14. F
15. O

Getting Personal (page 82)

Answers will vary.

Unbelievable Ads (page 83)

1. <u>Facts underlined</u>—In a blind taste test . . . Our chocolate chip cookies have chips that melt in your mouth. They are chewy and fit right in your hand. You can even microwave them and keep them warm.
   <u>Opinions circled</u>—Everybody loves the Yum!Yum! brand chocolate chip cookies. The stores sell out of them as soon as they arrive. The best tasting cookies you can buy.
2. <u>Facts underlined</u>—save three hundred dollars, comes complete with . . ., fifteen pre-installed games
   <u>Opinions circled</u>—speed can't be beat, everyone agrees . . ., deserves to win the Cool Computer Award, kids around the world are adding it to their wish list, best computer ever created.

You Be the Judge (page 84)

Answers may vary. Possible answers include:
Fact Farley—3, 6, 7, 8, 10
Opinion Opie—1, 2, 4, 5, 9

Winner: Fact Farley

TV Guide Budget (page 85)

Answers will vary.

Book Summary (page 86)

1. The Wisdom of Ponies
2. Keeping in Touch by E-mail
3. Eyes of the Twister
4. I Remember When
5. The Golden Rule Revolution
6. The Muskrat Mysteries

So Short (page 87)

Answers will vary.

In or Out? (page 88)

1. I
2. O
3. O
4. O
5. I
6. O
7. I
8. I

Match Time (page 89)

1. i
2. g
3. h
4. e
5. j
6. b
7. a
8. c
9. d
10. f

What's the Problem? (page 90)

Answers will vary.

What's Your Solution? (page 91)

Answers will vary.

The Best Solution (page 92)

1. b
2. d
3. d
4. a
5. d
6. c

Whose Views? (page 93)

Answers will vary.

Everyone Has a Different View (page 94)

Answers will vary.

Who Said That? (page 95)

Across

1. Cinderella
2. Baby bear
3. Wilbur
4. Prince
5. Wolf
8. Dorothy

Down

4. Pinocchio
6. Red Riding Hood
7. Charlotte
9. Goldilocks

Put Yourself in Other People's Shoes (page 96)

Answers will vary.

First or Third Person? (page 97)

1. Third
2. Third
3. First
4. Third
5. First
6. First
7. First
8. Third
9. First
10. First

What did you notice? Responses will vary but should mention that the words "I," "me," and "my" indicate first person point of view.

Cool Careers (page 98)

must graduate from college—teacher, vet
helps people—all
helps animals—vet
dangerous job—police
saves lives—police, vet
needs special training—all
needs special equipment—all
something you'd enjoy: answers will vary

Images (page 99)

Anwers wil vary. Possible answers include:
Picture 1–13 cats, 4 cats in the basket, no boys have striped shirts
Picture 2–11 cats, 3 cats in the basket, one boy wearing a striped shirt
Both–6 people, kids are carrying cats, 3 cats are playing by one boy's leg

Common Things (page 100)

Answers will vary.

Layers of Earth (page 101)

Answers will vary.

Many Connections (page 102)

1. book-to-self
2. book-to-book
3. book-to-self / book-to-world
4. book-to-world / book-to-self
5. book-to-world
6. book-to-self
7. book-to-world

Character Chains (page 103)

Answers will vary. Possible answers include:
both young females, both wandering in forest alone, both had poor manners, both encountered animals (wolf or bear,) both ate food

Similar Settings (page 104)

Pictures will vary.
Answers will vary. Possible answers include: both have little people, both have lollipops, both have brilliant colors, both

have crazy items that don't exist, both were imaginative, both involved factories

Book-to-Self Connections (page 105)
Answers will vary.

Book-to-World Connections (page 106)
Answers will vary.

Deduction Puzzle: Working Pigs (page 107)
Colby—construction worker
Shanelle—file clerk
Combo—waiter/waitress
Shasty—ice cream clerk

Deduction Puzzle: Forgetful Friends (page 108)
Fred—ruler
Frannie—homework
Froid—pencil
Frita—book

Inference Ice Cream (page 109)
Answers may vary. Possible answers include:
1. watermelon
2. mouse
3. duck
4. suitcase
5. Mars
6. snow
7. water

Movie Mania (page 110)
Answers may vary. Most likely answers include:
1. comedy
2. action
3. adventure
4. adventure
5. scary movie
6. adventure
7. comedy
8. cartoon

Mystery of the Missing Peanuts (page 111)
1. school—class, experiment, recess
2. the peanuts were missing
3. afternoon or after school—after recess and still hoping to do the experiment
4. squirrel probably took them to its hiding place in the trees
5. fall, grass, trees, country

Interesting Inferences (page 112)
1. she crashed her bike
2. birthday
3. roller coaster
4. snowing or hailing
5. Halloween trick-or-treating
6. tennis game

Word Choice (page 113)
1. It's
2. passed
3. capital
4. There
5. roll
6. than
7. already
8. weather
9. principal
10. fewer
11. lose
12. aisle

Make the Right Choice (page 114)
1. She should ask for a raise.
2. Please lay your things in your room.
3. Dessert will be an apple and a cookie.
4. Please remember to be quiet in the library.

Which Is Correct? (page 115)
1. I
2. C
3. C
4. C
5. I
6. C
7. I
8. C
9. C
10. I
11. I
12. C
13. C
14. I

Definition Match (page 116)
1. l
2. h
3. j
4. e
5. a
6. g
7. f
8. b
9. k
10. d
11. i
12. c